CliffsNotes®
Parent's
Crash Course™

ELEMENTARY SCHOOL
SCIENCE FAIR
PROJECTS

CliffsNotes®

Parent's *Crash Course*™

ELEMENTARY SCHOOL
SCIENCE FAIR PROJECTS

Faith Hickman Brynie

WILEY

Wiley Publishing, Inc.

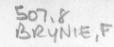
CliffsNotes® Parent's Crash Course™ Elementary School Science Fair Projects

Published by:
Wiley Publishing, Inc.
111 River Street
Hoboken, NJ 07030-5774
www.wiley.com

For general information on our other products and services or to obtain technical support please contact our Customer Care Department within the U.S. at (800) 762-2974, outside the U.S. at (317) 572-3993 or fax (317) 572-4002.

Wiley also publishes its books in a variety of electronic formats. Some content that appears in print may not be available in electronic books. For more information about Wiley products, please visit our web site at www.wiley.com.

Library of Congress Cataloging-in-Publication Data:
Brynie, Faith Hickman, 1946–
 CliffsNotes parent's crash course elementary school science fair projects / Faith Hickman Brynie.
   p.cm.
 ISBN-13: 978-0-7645-9934-7 (pbk.)
 ISBN-10: 0-7645-9934-8 (pbk.)
1. Science projects. 2. Science--Study and teaching (Elementary) I. Title: Parent's elementary school science fair projects. II. Title: Elementary school science fair projects. III. Title.
 Q182.3.B789 2006
 507'.8--dc22
                                    2005020233
Printed in the United States of America

10 9 8 7 6 5 4 3 2 1

Book design by Elizabeth Brooks
Cover design by José Almaguer
Book production by Wiley Publishing, Inc. Composition Services

Table of Contents

Introduction

Often parents are called upon to help their school-aged children with their homework, and just as often the parents have been removed from the subject matter for so long that they need to refamiliarize themselves with the basics of the material. That's what the *Parent's Crash Course* series is about.

Every school year—usually in the spring—millions of elementary school children complete science projects. Sometimes they present their projects only to their teacher and classmates. In other cases, school building, school district, city, regional, or even state science fairs or competitions are involved. Some assignments ask students to work as individuals, while others encourage partnerships or teamwork. Whatever the context, the basic requirement of all science projects is the same: Ask a real-world question and try to answer it using scientific methods of investigation.

For children and parents who get most of their science from the printed page or TV sound bites, science fair projects can be a daunting experience. Even eager parents willing to help may be as stymied as the child in deciding what to investigate and how. Add to that the demands of having a project due in a few days (when weeks or months are needed to do the job right), and even the happiest household can feel the strain.

Does the following exchange sound familiar?

"Mom," (drag that word out into a plaintive whine and read it as "Dad," if appropriate) "will you help me with my science project?"

"Sure. When's it due?" (You're calm, cool at this point, but you can feel your heartbeat quickening.)

"Next week."

"Next week?" you reply. (Read that with a gulp and a note of desperation). "I need a crash course in science projects!"

Well, here it is.

Part 1
Getting Started

Why Do a Science Project?

For many parents and their children, the goals of a science project may be unclear. You may wonder why it was assigned in the first place. The answer is threefold. Science projects are assigned so that the student can

- Explore a science topic in depth
- Assume responsibility for planning and carrying out a long-term endeavor
- Use scientific methods in seeking an answer to a real-world question

Beyond that, however, lie some important intellectual goals that may not be obvious to either parents or their children, the most important of which is this:

Science projects help students develop habits of thought that will serve them well in whatever activities or vocation they pursue, whether science-related or not.

A science project is something like a workout at the gym, but it's the mental muscles that grow. The workout begins with the warm-up: "What questions interest me?" "What question can I answer using experimental methods?" Then comes the hard work, when the pulse quickens and sweat pours. Materials must be gathered and organized into an experimental setup. Variables must be identified and controlled. Data must collected and analyzed—not once, but several times to assess the consistency of outcomes and discern average tendencies. From those data, logical conclusions must be drawn, and a poster or exhibit that explains the whole process must be constructed. Then comes the time when cooling down is required, but may be difficult to achieve: The project must be presented to others.

Throughout this process, mental muscles are at work that can grow flabby when school learning comes mostly from textbooks. A science project requires students (and the parents who assist them) to extract answers from nature—that is, to infer from their own observations how a natural process works. Achieving that end requires careful observation, description, classification, and measurement. The experimental process yields outcomes that are nearly always mathematical. To gain insight from them, students make data tables to organize results and draw graphs in hopes of revealing the trends that hide in raw numbers. But graphs cannot speak for themselves. They speak through the student experimenter who must interpret them logically. That's no small challenge, because the precise statement of what experimental results show—or don't show!—is a mental workout all on its own. Scientists say their craft requires healthy skepticism, which means being suspicious of pat answers and rejecting any conclusion not clearly and totally supported by all available evidence.

A science project is like a workout in one other way. Each project yields some benefit. Mind, like body, grows a little tougher, and the thinking muscles feel a tingle after exertion. But one workout is never enough. Growing stronger and staying strong require regular, vigorous exercise. That's why there's a science project next year and the year after that. Students should view future projects not as chores, but as opportunities. That's why science projects are never finished. Each one is preparation for the next, and the process of thinking, working, and acting scientifically is ongoing. That's why science projects are so important.

What Must a Science Project Contain?

First, consider what a science project is *not*.

- It is not reading from a textbook or studying for a test.
- It is not a reprise of an experiment done in science class, nor should it be drawn from any textbook.
- It's not a book report, scrapbook, term paper, or speech.
- Although many science fairs require a literature review on what is already known on the student's question, a science project is not a library or Internet research project on an assigned topic.
- A science fair project is not "learning the scientific method." It is acting as a scientist does: looking for a tangible way to gather evidence about how natural systems and processes function.

In short, a science fair project requires a student to ask an original question and look for an answer in a systematic, logical, and rigorous fashion.

Every science fair organizer—whether an individual classroom teacher or the committee that oversees a prestigious national or international competition—devises a comprehensive set of rules. Therefore, the first step in planning any science project is to find out exactly what those rules are and follow them to the letter. Although guidelines vary, you may find that your project should include the following components:

- **Title:** The title grows out of the question the project investigates. It can be the question itself or a declarative statement derived from it. Sometimes, fair organizers encourage clever titles as a way of heightening interest, but puns and riddles may be frowned on in other cases.
- **Goal (or Objective):** In this section, the student investigator states what he or she hoped to achieve in the project. The goal is a natural extension of the question. If the title sounds general, the goal statement is more specific.
- **Literature Review:** This is a summary of what is already known about a topic, derived from written research reports. The literature review should not be too long; that is, it should not summarize everything that is known about a topic, only what has been written about the specific question that the student experimenter seeks to answer.
- **Materials:** This is a list of all the equipment and supplies used in the project. Omit nothing.
- **Methods:** This is a step-by-step list of every action that was taken to set up an experiment and collect data. Again, omit nothing.
- **Results:** Here, the student presents all the data that were collected using the materials and methods described. These are the data tables and graphs that result from the observations and measurements collected throughout the experimental phase of the project.

- **Conclusions (or Discussion):** In this section, the student experimenter explains what the data mean by analyzing the evidence with a skeptical and critical eye. The data may support one interpretation, but not another. Or (and it takes a brave and honest investigator to state this), the results may be inconclusive. In such cases, as scientists frequently assert, "more research is needed."

- **Acknowledgments:** List the names and institutional affiliations of people who provided assistance and tell how they helped.

- **Bibliography (or References):** The list of sources cited in the literature review. Every fair has its own guidelines for the format to use in citing references. Check yours.

All this material comes from a journal or logbook that the student keeps throughout the project. Like a diary, it should begin on Day 1, when the project is first considered. In dated entries, the student records in the logbook all ideas, sources, observations, materials, successes, and failures—everything that the student investigator thinks about and everything that happens. Some fairs require submission of the logbook as part of the project, but even if submission is not required, the logbook is invaluable to the student experimenter. Things are less easily overlooked, forgotten, or lost if everything is recorded in a logbook.

Judged science fairs involving more than a single classroom of students often require both a display (often, a poster) and a written report. In advance of the fair, organizers typically ask that each entrant submit an abstract. The abstract is a one-page summary of the required sections listed above. Science fairs usually have specific size requirements for displays, and many require students to stand with their projects to present their work or answer questions from the judges. This is the acid test. Judges can tell immediately how eagerly a student has approached a project and how much he or she has learned from it.

Part 2
Project Ideas

How to Use the CliffNotes Science Fair Project Ideas

Included in Part II of this book are 60 project ideas that can help parents and children start on a meaningful science project. Each of these ideas provides a quick and easy—yet thought-provoking—opportunity for a science student to ask a question and look for an answer. These ideas are not (as some other books provide) canned and complete recipes to be followed, cookbook style. Instead, these simple beginnings are meant to lead students and their adult partners-in-learning into new territory, where inquiry is open and where each answer prompts a new and exhilarating question.

These ideas differ from the project plans presented in many other science fair books and online sources in three important ways. First, they work. That is not a matter to take lightly. Many investigations that look good on paper or on a Web site fail to deliver observable results. That won't happen with these ideas. Every one has been tried, tested, and perfected. You *will* get results. However—and this second difference is important—you will not find in these pages a ready-made conclusion, revealing either the expected results or the accepted explanation. Investigations in science should be true explorations for the students who pursue them and for the adults who assist. Knowing ahead of time what is supposed to happen impoverishes the experience.

Third, every idea points toward a controlled experiment. Each one employs what children often understand as a *fair test*. A question is posed, and a situation is constructed in which all factors that might influence the outcome are held constant except the one of interest. Toward this end, students should make sure they understand what variables are and how they are used in designing experiments:

- **Controlled variables:** All extraneous factors that can affect an outcome. The student experimenter makes sure the controlled variables are the same in all setups and trials of the experiment.
- **Independent variable:** The *single* variable of interest. The variable the student experimenter purposely changes to see if it has an effect.
- **Dependent variable:** The outcome that is observed or measured to see whether the independent variable made a difference. If a change occurs, it must be the result of the independent variable, because all other variables were kept the same.

Every experiment has at least two setups. One is the *control*. It is the setup that serves as a basis for comparison. Usually, nothing is done to the control. It is left as is, so that any differences observed between it and other setups must be the result of the treatment. For example, in one experiment, a science student might want to see whether lemon juice slows the browning of cut fruit slices. The experimental setup might be an apple slice dipped in lemon juice. The control might then be a similar slice left in air, one dipped in plain water, or both. The color of the dipped slice could later be compared to the control(s) to see whether the lemon juice made a difference.

In most science fair competitions, true experiments with carefully controlled and manipulated variables are rated more highly than model building, library research, or devices that merely demonstrate a known principle. However, there is more to gain from the experimental approach than simply the judges' favor. Designing and carrying out fair tests help children understand cause-and-effect relationships and draw valid, logical conclusions from all their experiences—whether science-related or not.

This book is organized to help parents and students identify a question, design and carry out an experiment, and complete a display in days, not weeks. That does not mean the CliffNotes science fair project ideas are either trivial or limited. In Part II, you'll find topics and questions that are important in science and important to a student's broadening understanding of the physical world. The ideas are arranged by topic areas, so a child can choose a subject of personal interest. More important, this book can grow with a child, because each idea offers numerous options for students and adults alike. So a simple project undertaken this year can lead to a more ambitious project at some future time.

Each idea begins with a question and some ideas parents can discuss with children ages 5 to 12. Then comes a list of materials. Most of the equipment and supplies are already in your kitchen junk drawer or the garage tool chest. If not, you can easily find most of them in discount houses, drugstores, or super-markets. If something might be tricky to locate, we've marked it in the materials list with an asterisk (*). You'll find full information on recommended brands and sources of the asterisk-marked items in the "Sources of Materials" chapter in Part III. For some projects, you may want to order something from a science supply house. You'll find addresses, phone numbers, and Web sites in the "Science Suppliers" chapter in Part III.

Following the materials list, the presentation continues with a section marked "Go." That section gives a step-by-step guide to a quick, simple experiment that most children around ages 8 or 9 can follow easily, building from a base of what they have already learned at home or in school.

However, children who are younger or are beginners with a topic can skip the "Go" option and move directly to "Go Easy." Under that heading is a simple project that primary-grade children can complete successfully in a short time. It's a good place to start, but student experimenters shouldn't forget that they can return to the "Go" section for next year's project.

On the other hand, if your child is older or is already knowledgeable on a topic, he or she may move immediately to the section called "Go Far." These more advanced ideas may be pursued as written, or they may stimulate students to formulate new, original ideas that are uniquely their own.

For many students, the options correspond to grade levels:

Grades K through 2: **GO EASY**

Grades 3 and 4: **GO**

Grades 5 and above: **GO FAR**

However, the project idea you and your child use together should depend less on the student's age or grade level and more on your child's knowledge, interests, and capabilities. And one other reminder: A project that begins as a last-minute effort now may grow into a substantial and important effort the next time a science project opportunity arises.

What Makes Honey Crystallize?

TALK IT OVER:

Have you ever noticed that honey crystallizes in a jar when you leave it in the cupboard for a long time? What is crystallization? What might make it happen faster?

GET:

- 5 small containers
- Stick-on labels and pen
- Cotton ball
- Vegetable oil
- Measuring spoons
- Honey
- Water
- Toothpick
- Freezer
- Kitchen timer
- Digital instant-read thermometer*

GO

1. Make five labels marked 0, 1, 2, 3, and 4. Attach one label to each of the five containers.

2. Dip the cotton ball in oil. Use it to wipe the inside of a measuring tablespoon. (This will make the honey slide out of the measuring spoon easily.)

3. Measure 1 tablespoon of honey into each of the five containers. To keep your measurements accurate, wipe the inside of the spoon with the oily cotton ball after each measurement.

4. To the container labeled 1, add 1 teaspoon of water. Add 2 teaspoons of water to the container marked 2, 3 teaspoons to container 3, and 4 teaspoons to container 4. To the container marked 0, add no water. It will contain only honey.

5. With a toothpick, stir the honey and water in each container until well mixed. Stir the honey in container 0 so it gets the same stirring treatment as the mixtures.

6. Put the containers together on a shelf in the freezer. Set the timer for 2 minutes.

7. After 2 minutes, open the freezer and check the containers for signs of crystals. If you see crystals in any one of the containers, take the temperature of the container's contents with the digital thermometer.

8. Keep timing and checking every 2 minutes. Measure temperatures in each container when you first see crystals forming.

9. Make notes of anything else you observe, including how long it takes for the contents of each container to crystallize completely.

STAY SAFE:

Pour the honey from the jar into the measuring spoon. Don't put the spoon into the honey jar. You'll get oil in the honey and spoil it for eating. Also, don't taste or eat the honey you use for this experiment.

GO EASY

Put 2 tablespoons of honey in one container. Put 1 tablespoon of honey mixed with 1 tablespoon of water in another. Put both in the freezer and observe every 2 minutes. Write down how long each takes to form crystals.

GO FAR

- Obtain several different kinds of honey, including clover honey and orange flower honey. Measure and compare the temperatures at which pure samples of each begin to crystallize.
- Test other sugar solutions using the "Go" procedure. You might try molasses, maple syrup, and corn syrup. Note similarities and differences and try to explain them.

SHOW YOUR RESULTS:

Record times in a table like this for "Go Easy":

Material Tested	Time It Took to Crystallize
Honey	
Honey and water	

Make a bar graph that compares crystallization time for pure honey and honey mixed with water.

For "Go," use a table like this:

Amount of Water (Added to 1 Tbsp. of Honey)	Time When Crystals First Appear (Minutes)	Temperature (°C) When Crystals First Appear
0		
1 tsp.		
2 tsp.		
3 tsp.		
4 tsp.		

Use your table to make a bar or line graph of water content (on the horizontal axis) and time to crystallization (on the vertical). Make a separate graph for the temperature of crystallization.

For "Go Far," make bar graphs comparing the crystallization temperature of different kinds of honey or different sugary solutions. Collect data and make a line graph that a friend could use to figure out the water content of any honey solution, knowing only the temperature at which crystals first appear.

Tips and Tricks

- Don't use a digital thermometer from the health section of your pharmacy or discount store. It is designed to measure human body temperatures and won't read low enough for this experiment. Choose a thermometer from the kitchen department. It will measure temperatures to freezing and below.

- Many thermometers read temperatures in both Fahrenheit (°F) and Celsius (°C). You can use either for this experiment; just be careful not to confuse them. If you want to work as scientists do, use °C.

- Keep the tip of the thermometer in the liquid. If it touches the container, you won't get an accurate reading.

- This is a good experiment to repeat several times. Averages of your times and temperatures over several trials are better than the results of a single trial alone.

Do Thick Liquids Flow Faster or Slower Than Thin Ones?

TALK IT OVER:

Liquids flow or run over surfaces—you notice that when you spill them. Do some liquids flow faster or farther than others? Does how thick or thin they are make a difference?

GET:

- Piece of glass (glass from a large picture frame works well)
- Glass cleaner and dry cloth
- Ruler
- Books

- Liquids for testing, such as molasses, vegetable oil, vinegar, and water
- Droppers (a clean dropper for each liquid)
- Stopwatch or clock with a second hand

GO

1. Clean the glass with the glass cleaner and cloth.
2. Measure the length of the glass plate with the ruler. This is the distance your liquids will travel. Record this number.

3. Set one or more books on your work surface. Set an end of the glass on the books, like this:

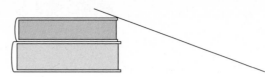

4. Pull a little of the liquid you want to test into a clean dropper.

5. Quickly drop 5 drops of the liquid onto the glass plate at its high point. Immediately start the stopwatch (or note the time on the clock with a second hand).

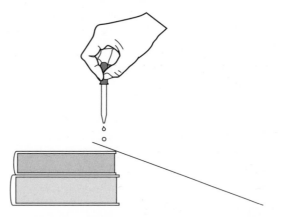

6. When the stream of liquid reaches the bottom of the glass, stop the stopwatch (or note the elapsed time). Record how long the liquid took to reach the bottom of the glass.

7. Clean the glass and repeat steps 3–6 twice more with the same liquid.

8. Calculate and record the average travel time for this liquid:

$$\frac{\text{Trial 1} + \text{Trial 2} + \text{Trial 3}}{3} = \text{average}$$

9. Clean the glass and repeat steps 3–8 with each of the liquids you wish to test.

STAY SAFE:

Careful with the glass plate. Its edges may be sharp.

GO EASY

Use the "Go" procedure to compare only two liquids, a thick liquid like maple syrup and a thin liquid like water. Get an adult's help with measuring, timing, and averaging.

GO FAR

Viscosity is the resistance of a liquid to flow. Thick liquids have high viscosity. Thin liquids have low viscosity. Use the "Go" procedure to compare the viscosity of several liquids. Calculate and compare the rate of travel for the liquids in centimeters per second using this formula:

distance traveled (length of glass in centimeters) ÷ time of travel in seconds = cm/sec

You might also try comparing the viscosity of different brands of maple syrup or different weights of motor oil.

SHOW YOUR RESULTS:

Put travel times in a data table like this for "Go Easy":

Liquid Tested	Travel Time Trial 1	Travel Time Trial 2	Travel Time Trial 3	Average Travel Time
Maple syrup				
Water				

For "Go," use the same data table, adding a row for each liquid you test. Make a bar graph that compares travel times.

For "Go Far," make a bar graph that compares your calculated values of distance traveled per second. Make graphs to show the results of any other experiment you conduct.

Tips and Tricks

- Make sure you clean and dry the glass thoroughly between each trial. Dirty glass will affect your results.
- If 5 drops are too much (the liquid travels too fast) or too little (the liquid travels too slowly), decrease or increase the amount. Just make sure you use the same amount in all tests of all liquids or your comparisons will not be valid.
- If your liquids are traveling too slowly or quickly, try using more or fewer books to raise or lower the starting point.

What's the Best Way to Get Stains Out of Clothes?

TALK IT OVER:

What kinds of things stain your clothes? How do you get stains out? Do some stain removers work better than others?

GET:

- Old white T-shirt
- Ruler
- Scissors
- Large, shallow pan
- Purple grape juice
- Spoon
- Masking tape
- Waterproof marker or ballpoint pen

- Staple gun and staples
- Cookie sheet
- Possible stain removers to test, such as laundry detergent, bath soap, dishwashing liquid, bleach, or commercial stain removal preparations
- Droppers

GO

1. From the T-shirt, cut square pieces 10 cm x 10 cm (4" x 4"). Cut a piece for each stain removal preparation you want to test, plus two extras.

2. Put the pieces of T-shirt in the pan. Spread them out. Pour in enough purple grape juice to cover them. Stir them well, so that all the pieces get thoroughly soaked. Let them sit overnight.

3. Remove the pieces and squeeze out the excess grape juice. Let the pieces dry completely.

4. Using a waterproof marker or ballpoint pen, make masking tape labels for each stain removal product you want to test. Make two extra labels: "Water" and "Control." Staple the labels to the T-shirt pieces.

5. Spread the pieces on a cookie sheet. Using a clean dropper, put 10 drops of water on the center of the piece labeled "Water." Put nothing on the "Control" piece.

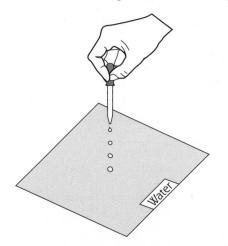

6. Using a clean dropper for each stain remover, put 10 drops of the product on the center of its labeled piece. If you are using a solid such as bar soap or a stain removal stick, rub a small amount onto the center of the piece. Allow all samples to dry.

7. Put all the pieces in a pan of clear water. Soak overnight. Remove and allow to dry.

8. Examine the spots in the centers of the pieces. Arrange the pieces in order, from the piece that shows the most stain removal to the piece that shows the least. (Compare the product pieces to the "Water" and "Control" pieces.) Assign numbers, using 1 for the best stain remover, 2 for the second best, and so on.

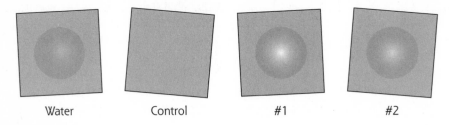

| Water | Control | #1 | #2 |

STAY SAFE:

Ask an adult for help if you test bleach or any other strong household cleaner. Such products can burn your skin and sting your eyes. Handle droppers carefully. Wash and rinse them immediately after use.

GO EASY

Test a commercial stain remover against plain water. Describe the difference you see.

GO FAR

Test a variety of stain removal products using different stains. You might try ketchup, butter, grass stains, chocolate, and more. Test different fabrics such as wool, cotton, and polyester. Or, you might want to test different brands of laundry detergent for their stain-removing power.

SHOW YOUR RESULTS:

For "Go Easy," display your pieces, describe your results, and draw a conclusion about the stain-removal ability of the product you tested.

For "Go," display your samples in a table like this, putting the best stain remover at the top (rank 1) and the worst at the bottom:

Rank	Product Tested	Samples
1		
2		
3 . . . and so on		

For "Go Far," make a separate table for each of the stains, fabrics, or detergents you tested.

Tips and Tricks

Step 7 of the "Go" procedure makes this a fair test, because all the stain-removal preparations are subjected to the same treatment. You might want to try another experiment, though, following the manufacturer's washing directions for each product and comparing the results.

Which Brand of Soap Releases the Most Water Quickly?

TALK IT OVER:

Soap is partly water. In a microwave oven, water heats quickly and makes steam. What might happen to soap in the microwave? How can you use the microwave to find out how quickly a soap gives up water?

GET: _____

- 2 or more bars of soap, different brands
- 2 or more microwave-safe plates (not paper or plastic)
- Kitchen scale
- Hot pad
- Access to a microwave oven

1. Weigh a plate on the kitchen scale. Put a bar of soap on the plate and weigh again.

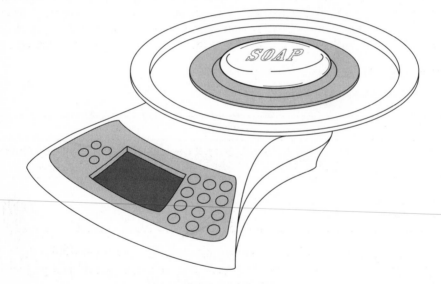

2. Repeat step 1 for each brand of bar soap you want to test.
3. One at a time, place the bars of soap in the microwave oven. Heat on high power for 1 minute. Using the hot pad, remove the plate and soap from the oven.
4. Cool completely.
5. Weigh each plate along with its soap again.
6. In order to compare bars of soap that did not start out weighing the same, you'll need to calculate *percent change*. Here's how:
   a. Calculate the weight of the bar of soap before and after microwaving. To get the weight of the bar of soap:

   (weight of soap + plate) – (weight of plate) = weight of soap
   b. Calculate the change (the amount of water that left the soap):

weight of soap after − weight of soap before = change in weight

  c. Percent change equals

  (change in weight ÷ weight of soap before) × 100 = percent change

STAY SAFE:

Do not touch the soap after it has been in the microwave. It gets very hot. Also, do not microwave for more than 1 minute. Some soaps get hot enough to crack even microwave-safe plates.

GO EASY

Ask an adult to help you with the microwaving and the calculations. Talk about what *percent change* means and how your numbers compare.

GO FAR

This experiment works because microwaves heat water molecules. They make the molecules move faster. As the water molecules heat, they change their *physical state:* from liquid water into gaseous water vapor. The vapor expands and leaves the soap, moving into the air. You can use this idea and the "Go" procedure to test other materials for their water content. Try comparing meats, vegetables, or different types of cheese. Make sure whatever you test is safe to put in the microwave.

SHOW YOUR RESULTS:

Put weights and calculations in a data table like this:

Weights						
Brand of Soap	Plate	Plate + Soap (Before)	Soap Only (Before)	Plate + Soap (After)	Soap Only (After)	Percent Change
Brand X						
Brand Y . . . and so on						

Make a bar graph that compares the percent change of different brands. Put the brands on the horizontal axis. Put percent change on the vertical. Display your soaps as part of your project. State a conclusion about which brand of soap loses water most quickly.

Tips and Tricks

- A triple-beam balance borrowed from your school's science lab will give you more accurate weights than a kitchen scale will.
- The change in the weight of the soap is the amount of water lost. Expand your experiment by measuring the amount of water lost in 15-second intervals of microwaving. Is it always the same, or does the soap lose more water early in the heating process than later?

How Much Fat Is in Potato Chips?

TALK IT OVER:

Have you ever noticed greasy spots on the sides of paper bags containing certain foods? What is fat in foods? How do you know it is there? How can you tell whether some foods contain more fat than others do?

GET:

- Several brands of potato chips
- Graph paper, ¼-inch ruled, 1 piece for each brand of chips
- Wax paper
- Rolling pin
- Towel
- Window
- Tape
- Grease pencil

GO

1. Place a potato chip on a piece of graph paper.
2. Place a piece of wax paper over it.
3. Roll with a rolling pin, crushing the chip between the wax paper and the graph paper. Roll long and hard until the chip is thoroughly crushed.

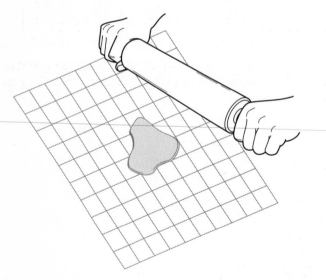

4. Remove the graph paper. Wipe it with a towel to get rid of little pieces of chip that cling to the paper.
5. Tape the graph paper to a window. Notice that the paper is translucent in some places. (*Translucent* means that it lets light through. The greasy spot the chip left is translucent.) Record your observations.

6. Count the number of squares on the graph paper that are translucent. Any square that is one-half or more translucent counts as a whole square. Mark the squares with the grease pencil as you go, so that you can keep count.

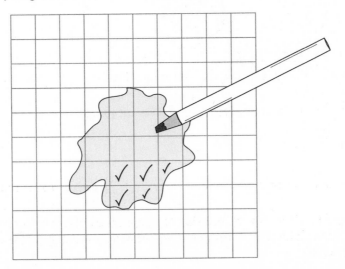

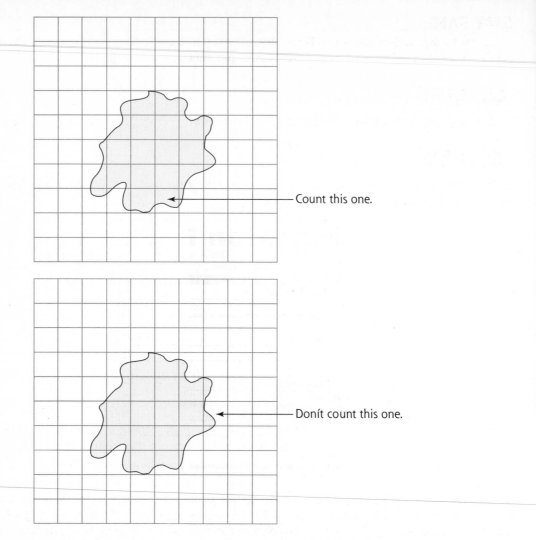

Count this one.

Don't count this one.

7. Repeat steps 1 through 6 twice more, using the same brand of chip. This will give you three trials to average.

8. Repeat steps 1–7 for each brand of potato chip you want to test.

STAY SAFE:

Hang on to that rolling pin—you'll say "Ouch!" if you drop it on your toe. Don't eat the chips you crush. Discard the chip crumbs and the wax paper sheets.

GO EASY

Follow the "Go" procedure, but omit step 7. Count translucent squares for only 1 chip of each brand.

GO FAR

Examine the nutrition label on the chip package. Find the approximate number of chips in 1 serving. Find the total number of fat grams per serving.

Nutrition Facts
Serving Size 1 oz. (28g/About 7 chips) ← Serving size
Servings Per Container 20

Amount Per Serving

Calories 140	Calories from Fat 60

	% Daily Value*
Total Fat 7g ← Fat in 1 serving	11%
Saturated Fat 1g	5%
Trans Fat 0g	
Cholesterol 0mg	0%
Sodium 120mg	5%
Total Carbohydrate 19g	6%
Dietary Fiber 1g	5%
Sugars 0g	
Protein 2g	

To find the grams of fat in one chip, divide the fat grams by the number of chips. For example, if one serving is 7 chips and the grams of fat is 10, the grams of fat per chip is 10 ÷ 7 = 1.43. Add the calculated fat value to your data table. This number should be *proportional* to the number of squares you counted. Is it?

If you want to extend this project, develop your own procedure for measuring the fat in milk, cheese, baked goods, or snack foods.

SHOW YOUR RESULTS:

For "Go Easy," use a data table like this:

Brand	Squares	Observations
A		
B		
C . . . and so on		

For "Go," your table should look like this:

Brand	Squares	Observations
A		
Trial 1		
Trial 2		
Trial 3		
Average		
B . . . and so on		
Trial 1		
Trial 2		
Trial 3		
Average		

For "Go Easy" and "Go," make a bar graph that compares numbers of translucent squares (on the vertical axis) by brand (on the horizontal axis). For "Go," use your average from three trials.

For "Go Far," add to the data table a column for the fat grams/chip value you calculated from the nutrition label. When you make your bar graph, set up two vertical axes. Put translucent squares per chip on a vertical axis on the left. Put fat grams per chip on a vertical axis on the right. Use different color bars to show how your measured and calculated values compare. Your graph will look something like this:

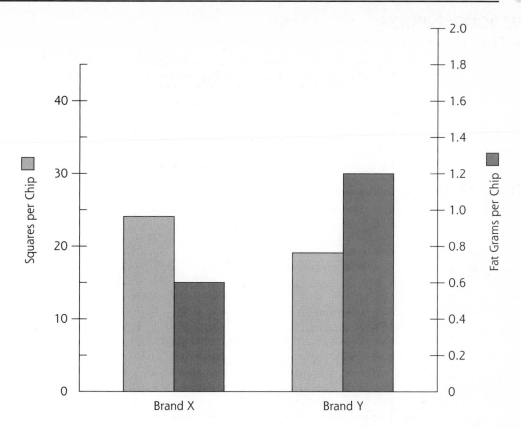

For "Go" and "Go Easy," write a few sentences about how the chips compare in their fat content. For "Go Far," add a discussion of how well your measured and calculated values compare. Try to explain why they are alike or different.

Tips and Tricks

When selecting chips to crush, choose unbroken chips of average size. Large, small, or damaged chips will give you imprecise measurements.

Are Household Powders Acids or Bases?

TALK IT OVER:

Many everyday substances are either acids or bases. Orange juice, vinegar, and cola drinks are acids. Many cleaners, such as household ammonia, are bases. Some substances, called *indicators*, are one color in an acid and another color in a base. You can use them to tell acids and bases apart.

GET:

- 1-cup measuring cup
- Rubbing alcohol
- Measuring spoon
- Ground turmeric (from the spice aisle at the supermarket)
- Spoons
- Sieve
- Coffee filter
- Small jam jar
- 1 gallon *distilled* water (available in the laundry products aisle at the supermarket)

- Plate
- Dropper
- Ziptop plastic sandwich bags
- Rolling pin
- Powders to test such as baking soda, baking powder, washing soda, salt, sugar, cream of tartar, chalk, Epsom salts, dishwasher powder, powder laundry detergent, borax, laundry soap, or pills such as calcium, vitamin C, antacids, or aspirin

GO

1. First, make an indicator from turmeric, following these steps:

   a. Measure ¼ cup of rubbing alcohol into the measuring cup.

   b. Add ¼ teaspoon ground turmeric.

   c. Stir well with a spoon.

   d. Put the sieve on top of the jar.

   e. Put the coffee filter in the sieve.

   f. Pour the alcohol/turmeric mixture through.

   g. When all the liquid has run through the coffee filter, remove the sieve and put the filter in the trash.

   h. Add ½ cup of distilled water to the alcohol/turmeric mixture in the jar. Stir.

   i. This is your turmeric indicator. It will turn an acid bright yellow. It will turn a base bright red.

2. To test a powder, use a clean, dry spoon to put a small amount of the powder on a plate. Using the dropper, add a few drops of your turmeric indicator and note the color change, if any. (If the indicator remains pale yellow, the powder is neither an acid nor a base.)

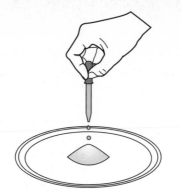

3. To test a pill, place it in a ziptop bag and roll with a rolling pin to crush it into a powder. Then test as in step 2.

STAY SAFE:

Rubbing alcohol is poisonous and can hurt your eyes. Do not use rubbing alcohol without an adult's help. Some cleaning powders can burn your skin. Never put any of the materials used in this experiment in your mouth or eyes. If you get some on your skin, wash with water immediately.

GO EASY

The "Go" procedure will work for you. Try testing three powders: dishwasher powder, salt, and baking soda.

GO FAR

Turmeric isn't the only useful indicator you can make at home. Boil some red cabbage in a small amount of water and use it to test powders. Relating it to your turmeric data, you should be able to infer what its color changes show. Purple grape juice and the packing juice from canned blueberries are worth a try also. Read more in the following project about the pH scale and how it is used to measure acids and bases. If time permits, order some pH paper from a scientific supply house or borrow some from your school. Use it to check the conclusions you drew from your indicator experiments.

SHOW YOUR RESULTS:

Put check marks in a data table like this for "Go Easy" and "Go":

Powder Tested	Acid	Base	Neither
Dishwasher powder			
Salt			
Baking soda . . . and so on			

Make a poster showing which of the powders you tested were acids and which were bases. Put your turmeric indicator and some test powders in your display so visitors can see the difference for themselves.

For "Go Far," make data tables and graphs that relate your results with different indicators to what you learned about the pH scale.

Tips and Tricks

- Be sure to use distilled water when you make your turmeric indicator. Some tap water is acidic or basic enough to change the color of your indicator before you start your powder tests.
- Do not get any powder on your dropper or in your indicator. If you do, you'll need to make fresh indicator.
- Make your own indicator paper. Cut strips from a coffee filter. Soak them in your turmeric indicator and let them dry. Then try dipping a strip in a liquid. If it turns red, the liquid is a base. If it turns bright yellow, the liquid is an acid.

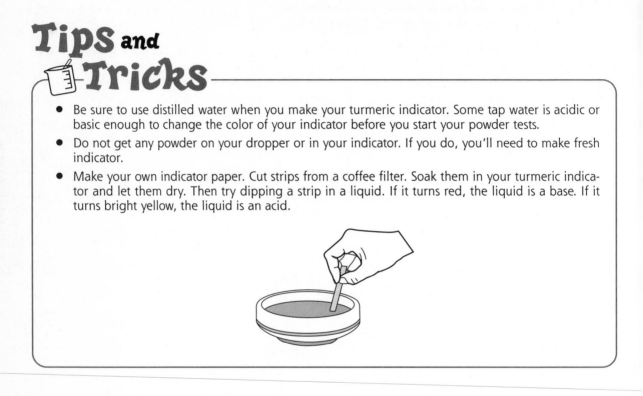

What Are the pH and Total Alkalinity of Personal Care Products?

TALK IT OVER:

When you use soaps, shampoos, and lotions, you want them to make your hair and body clean and your skin soft. You don't want irritations, rashes, or pimples. Scientists who develop skin and hair care products must control the chemistry of their products to make them both safe and effective. Two things that must be controlled are *pH* and *total alkalinity*.

People use a pH number to describe how *acidic* or *basic* a substance is. The pH scale goes from 0 to 14. A *neutral substance* (neither acidic nor basic) has a pH of 7.0. A pH value less than 7.0 indicates an *acid substance*. The lower the number, the more acidic the substance. A value higher than 7.0 is *a base substance,* or *basic.* The higher the number, the more basic the substance.

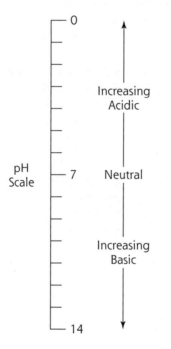

Total alkalinity is a measure of how *resistant* the product is to a change in pH. The higher its number, the more stable the pH value is.

GET: _____

- Pack of test strips for pH and total alkalinity (used for pools and spas)*
- Products to test such as shampoos, lotions, toners, shower gels, face creams, and others

GO

1. Study the color codes on the side of your test strip package. You should see color comparisons for both pH and total alkalinity, with numbers indicated. Note that most pool and spa test strips measure a narrow range of pH, often from 6.2 to 8.4. Total alkalinity is measured in parts per million (ppm), often from 0 to 240.

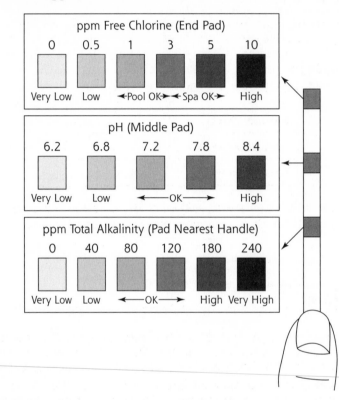

2. For each product you wish to test, put a drop or two on the color pads of the test strip.
3. Wait a minute, then compare the result to the color codes on the package. Record the name of the product, its pH, and the total alkalinity in your data table.

STAY SAFE:

Do not put test strips in your mouth. Do not taste personal care products. Dispose of test strips safely after use.

GO EASY

Do not test for total alkalinity. Make your project about pH only.

GO FAR

Try testing several different products within a single category such as shampoos or shower gels. Use your data to answer the following question: How much do different brands of a single kind of product (such as shampoos) vary? Average your data within categories, and use your averages to answer the following question: How much do different categories of products (such as shampoos and shower gels) vary from each other?

You might also want to use the "Go" procedure to compare other substances, such as soft drinks, household cleaners, medicines, or foods.

SHOW YOUR RESULTS:

Put test results in a data table like this for "Go Easy":

Product Tested	pH
Shiny shampoo	
Slinky shower soap . . . and so on	

For "Go" and "Go Far," add a column for total alkalinity. For all, make bar graphs to show how products and categories compare. Write a few sentences stating your conclusions.

Tips and Tricks

- If you don't quite understand pH, try this practical demonstration. Dip your test strip in lemon juice. Lemon juice is an acid. What does your strip show? Then dissolve an Alka-Seltzer table in water and test with a strip. Alka-Seltzer is a base. What does your test strip show?

- Note the limits that your test strips place on how you report your data. At the extremes of a test strip's range, you cannot be sure of the true value. For example, if your shampoo shows the color that indicates pH 8.4, you cannot be sure what the pH actually is. It might be higher than 8.4. So you must report pH 8.4 *or higher* in your data table. The same thing happens at the low end of the range. You'll need to report pH 6.2 *or lower*. For this reason, when buying your test strips, try to get the widest ranges of pH and total alkalinity values available.

How Do Acids and Bases Affect Enzyme Action?

TALK IT OVER:

Enzymes are substances in cells that make a chemical reaction go faster. Yeast cells have an enzyme in them called *catalase*. It causes hydrogen peroxide to break down into oxygen gas and water. How can you observe this reaction? How can you measure whether an acid like lemon juice or a base like baking soda affects the reaction?

GET:

- Glass or jar
- Measuring cup
- Measuring spoons
- Baking soda
- 1 gallon *distilled* water (available in the laundry products aisle of the supermarket)
- Spoons for stirring

- 5 straight-sided juice glasses
- Marker or labels
- Hydrogen peroxide
- Lemon juice
- Packet of dry yeast
- Ruler

GO

1. Into a glass or jar, place ½ cup of distilled water and ½ teaspoon of baking soda. Stir to dissolve.

2. Label the juice glasses 1–5. Add to them the substances shown in the table. Make sure you add the yeast last. Then stir *briefly* only to mix.

Glass	Hydrogen Peroxide	Lemon Juice	Baking Soda Solution (from Step 1)	Distilled Water	Yeast: Add Last
1 (control)	⅛ cup	none	None	2 tsp.	⅛ tsp.
2	⅛ cup	1 tsp.	None	1 tsp.	⅛ tsp.
3	⅛ cup	2 tsp.	None	none	⅛ tsp.
4	⅛ cup	none	1 tsp.	1 tsp.	⅛ tsp.
5	⅛ cup	none	2 tsp.	none	⅛ tsp.

3. Stand back and watch the glasses from the side. Make notes in your data table about what you see happening in each glass.

4. When the reaction appears to have stopped, measure and record the height of the bubbles in each glass, like this:

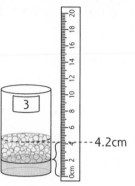

The bubbles give you a measure of how much oxygen gas was released.

STAY SAFE:

Don't drink hydrogen peroxide. Don't get it on your skin unless you know you are not allergic. Don't get it on your clothes, because it takes the color out of some fabrics.

GO EASY

Use only glasses 1, 3, and 5.

GO FAR

Set up more glasses and test other amounts of lemon juice and baking soda. Get some pH paper and measure the pH in each glass. How does pH relate to the height of the bubbles?

The reaction you saw is the result of enzyme action in yeast . . . or is it? See whether you can get similar results leaving out the yeast and using other small-grained additions such as fine sand or salt instead. Does added lemon juice or baking soda affect the height of bubbles in those setups? What can you conclude from comparing results?

SHOW YOUR RESULTS:

Put the heights of the bubbles in a data table like this for "Go Easy":

Glass	Bubble Height	Observations
1 (control)		
3		
5		

For "Go," add glasses 2 and 4 to the table. For both, make a bar graph that shows how the heights of the bubbles compare. Write a few sentences on how an acid (the lemon juice) and a base (the baking soda) affect the amount of gas released.

For "Go Far," add other mixtures and pH measurements to your table. Make separate tables for the yeast substitutes such as salt and fine sand. Use bar graphs to answer the following question: Are the bubbles produced by an enzyme in the yeast or by the physical action of fine grains?

Tips and Tricks

- Make sure you understand the importance of glass 1 and why it is set up the way it is. It is the basis for comparison for what happens in all the other glasses.
- You'll get results that are more reliable if you conduct each test several times and average the results.

Which Fruit Juice Has the Most Vitamin C?

TALK IT OVER:

Vitamin C is important to good health. Among other things, it helps fight off colds and flu. Which fruit juices should you drink to get the most vitamin C?

GET: _____

- Cornstarch
- Water
- Pot and stove
- Measuring spoons
- Measuring cup
- Water glasses

- Iodine solution* and a dropper
- Dropper that measures in milliliters*
- Some juices to test (pineapple, apple, grapefruit, orange, lemon, and so on)
- Paper cups
- Spoons for stirring

GO

1. Get an adult to do the cooking for you. Boil 4 cups of water in a pot. Add ¼ teaspoon cornstarch and stir to dissolve. Allow this solution to cool completely before going on to step 2.

2. Measure ¼ cup of the cornstarch and water mixture into a water glass. Add 8 drops of iodine. Stir. The mixture will turn dark blue.

3. Put some of the juice you want to test into a paper cup. Pull some of the juice into the milliliter dropper. Watching amounts carefully, start adding juice to the blue mixture 1 milliliter at a time. Count and keep track of the number of milliliters you add. Stir after every addition and look closely at the blue color. When it disappears, stop adding juice. Record the total number of milliliters of juice needed to get rid of the blue.

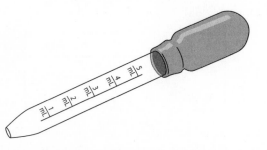

4. Repeat steps 2 and 3 for each juice you want to test. Always use clean glasses and spoons. Wash and dry your milliliter dropper between each test.

5. This experiment works because iodine molecules and starch molecules hook together in solution, causing the blue color. Vitamin C breaks them apart. So the *more* milliliters of a juice you add to make the blue disappear, the *less* vitamin C the juice contains.

STAY SAFE:

Make sure an adult does the cooking for you. Let the starch solution cool before you use it. Don't drink the iodine or the test solutions. If you get them on your skin, wash with soap and water. Don't get them on your clothes, because they will stain.

GO EASY

Following the "Go" procedure, test pineapple juice and apple juice only.

GO FAR

Perform three tests for each juice and average the results. Then use a standard solution that will let you determine exactly how much vitamin C is in each juice. To make your standard, crush a 250-milligram vitamin C tablet. Dissolve it in 250 milliliters (1 cup) of water. The concentration of your standard is then 250 milligrams/250 milliliters, or 1 mg/ml. Then follow the "Go" procedure, using the standard instead of a juice. This tells you how many milligrams of vitamin C you need to make the blue disappear. You can then calculate the milligrams of vitamin C in each of your juices using this formula:

ml of standard (needed to remove blue) ÷ ml of juice = mg of vitamin C per ml of juice

For example, if you needed 10 milliliters of the standard to get rid of the blue, and it took 20 milliliters of a juice to do it, the concentration of vitamin C in the juice is 10/20 or 0.5 mg/ml.

To expand your project, find out how heat, light, or storage time affects vitamin C content. Compare real juices with prepared soft drink mixes or canned sodas; or compare fresh or canned juices with frozen concentrates prepared according to the directions on the package.

SHOW YOUR RESULTS:

Put milliliters of juice in a data table like this for "Go" and Go Easy":

Juice	Milliliters
Pineapple	
Apple . . . and so on	

For "Go Far," add rows for three trials and a row for an average for each kind of juice. Also add a column showing your calculated value for the mg/ml concentration of each juice.

For all three projects, make bar graphs of the milliliters needed to make the blue disappear (on the vertical axis) by the name of the juice (on the horizontal axis). For "Go Far," use your average values from three trials to make the bar graph. Make a separate graph showing the mg/ml concentrations you calculated. Remember, when writing your conclusions, the *largest* milliliter counts are the juices with the *least* vitamin C.

Tips and Tricks

- If you experiment on more than one day, keep your cornstarch solution in the refrigerator. Shake it if the cornstarch settles.
- If you are doing multiple trials of the same juice, do them all at the same time. Storing your juices or using a different batch made up on another day may affect your results.
- To test grape juice, use the white kind. You can't see the color change in purple juice. Cola drinks and tomato juice are hard to test for the same reason.

Do Chemical Reactions Absorb or Release Energy?

TALK IT OVER:

When chemical changes happen, is there an energy change as well? Do some reactions give off heat while others absorb it? How can you find out?

GET: _____

- 4 juice glasses
- Vinegar
- Scissors
- Steel wool pad
- Packet of dry yeast
- Hydrogen peroxide
- Baking soda

- Epsom salts
- NoSalt salt alternative (contains potassium chloride)
- Water
- Small spoons
- Digital instant-read thermometer*
- Sink or plastic tub

GO

1. You will make the mixtures shown in the chart below one at a time. Here's how:

    a. Fill a clean juice glass about half full of the liquid shown in the left column.

    b. Take and record the temperature of the liquid.

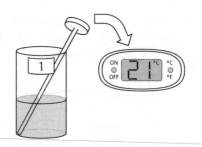

    c. Add to the liquid a little of the material shown in the right column.

    d. Wait 2 minutes or longer and take the temperature again. Record.

Mix This Reactant . . .	. . . With This Reactant
Vinegar	Baking soda
Water	Epsom salts
Vinegar	A steel wool pad (when the pad is well soaked with vinegar, pour off the excess)
Hydrogen peroxide	Dry yeast
Water	NoSalt salt alternative

2. Repeat the procedure for all five reactions. Use clean materials each time.

3. For each reaction, subtract to find the temperature change:

   ending temperature – starting temperature = temperature change

   If your answer is a + (positive) number, the liquid got hotter and the reaction released energy.

   If your answer is a – (negative) number, the liquid got colder and the reaction absorbed energy.

STAY SAFE:

Don't touch the glasses after the reactants are mixed. Some of them may get very warm. Control spills and fizz-overs by doing these experiments in a sink or plastic tub.

GO EASY

Try only two reactions: vinegar/steel wool and vinegar/baking soda. Ask an adult to help you calculate and understand positive and negative temperature changes.

GO FAR

Chemical reactions that release energy are *exothermic*. Reactions that absorb energy are *endothermic*. You can learn more about them using this procedure:

1. At your local drugstore, purchase instant cold packs and hot packs—the kind athletes use to relieve strains and sprains. Find a brand of cold pack that contains ammonium nitrate and water. Find a brand of hot pack that contains calcium chloride and water. You may want to try more than one size or brand.

2. For each kind of pack you want to test, put a measured amount of room temperature water in a pitcher or bucket. You want water deep enough to submerge the pack, but not much more.

3. Take the temperature of the water.

4. Activate the pack according to the directions on the package. Submerge the pack in the water. Hold it under the water's surface with a long-handled, wooden spoon, if you need to.

5. Start a stopwatch or timer and take the temperature of the water every minute.

6. How well do the packs work? Do some work better than others?

Note: Do not try this experiment with any electrical or battery-operated device. Do not open the packs or release the chemicals inside them. Dispose of them after use according to the directions on the package.

SHOW YOUR RESULTS:

Put temperatures and calculations in a data table like this for "Go" and "Go Easy":

Reactants Tested	Starting Temperature	Ending Temperature	Temperature Change
Vinegar/steel wool			
Vinegar/baking soda . . . and so on			

Make a bar graph showing the temperature change for each reaction. Put the names of the reactions on the horizontal axis. Because some of your temperature changes may be expressed in negative numbers, your vertical axis will extend both above and below the zero (0) point, like this:

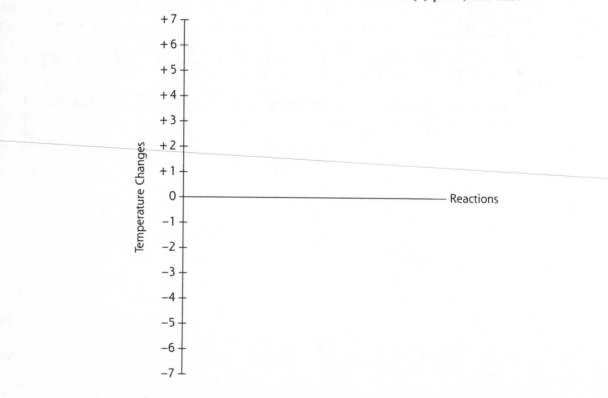

Write a few sentences telling which of your reactions absorbed energy and which released energy. Explain how your data support your conclusions.

For "Go Far," use a data table like this:

| Pack tested | Water Temperature | | | | | Temperature Change |
	0 Minutes (Before Pack Added)	1 Minute	2 Minutes	3 Minutes	And So On . . .	
Cold pack brand A						
Cold pack brand B						
Hot pack brand X . . . and so on						

Make a bar graph that compares types and brands of packs. Draw the conclusions about them that your data support.

Tips and Tricks

- You can often tell whether a reaction releases or absorbs energy by feeling the side of the glass. But do not put your finger in. Some reactions get hot enough to burn you!
- The hot and cold packs that you warm in the microwave or chill in the freezer are not chemical reactions. They rely on simple physical changes, because the grains or gels inside the packs remain the same substance when they warm or cool.

How Easily Do Objects Move over Surfaces?

TALK IT OVER:

Does it take more force to move an object over a smooth surface or a rough one? How can you find out?

GET:

- Small block of wood
- Drill
- Sandpaper
- 4 pieces of cardboard, about 8½ in. x 11 in.
- 3 new pieces of sandpaper: 1 each fine, medium, and coarse
- Glue stick
- Hole punch
- Paper cup
- String
- Table
- Paper clips

 GO

1. Ask an adult to drill a hole in the block of wood, close to a corner, like this:

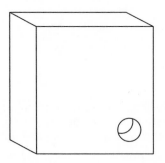

2. Sand rough edges smooth.

3. Glue the sandpaper pieces, one of each type, to a separate cardboard backing. Make sure the sandpaper is glued smooth and level. Leave the other piece of cardboard smooth.

4. Punch three holes in the paper cup. Thread strings through the holes and tie them like this, leaving one long piece:

5. Put the smooth cardboard piece on the edge of the table. Place the block of wood on the cardboard, like this:

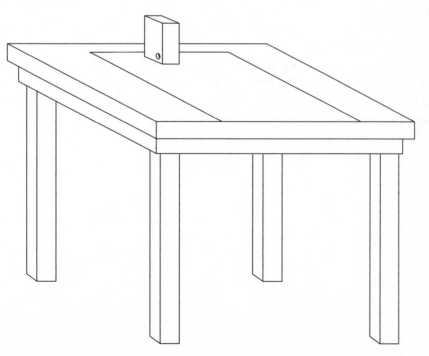

6. Tie the cup to the block with the string, letting the cup hang below the table's edge, like this:

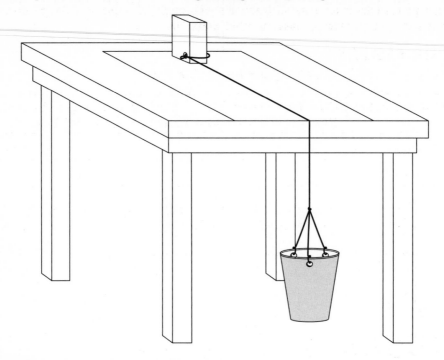

7. Start adding paper clips to the cup, one at a time, counting as you go. Record the number when the block first begins to move. Also record the number that moves the block the full length of the cardboard to the edge of the table.

8. Replace the smooth cardboard with a sandpaper-covered board, and repeat steps 5–7. Keep testing until you have collected data for the block's movement on all the boards.

STAY SAFE:
Handle sandpaper carefully. It can scratch your skin.

GO EASY
Test smooth cardboard against a single grade of sandpaper.

GO FAR

Friction is the force that resists the relative motion of objects that are in contact with each other. *Inertia* is an object's tendency to remain at rest or in motion. Inertia depends on the mass and shape of the object. You had to overcome inertia to get the block moving. You had to overcome friction as the block moved the length of the board. (In the "Go" procedure, you measured both forces in grams. Why? Because each paper clip has a mass of approximately 1 gram.)

Use the same method to measure and compare the inertia of other objects such as a small cardboard box, a stapler, a glue stick, or toy cars with wheels. You might also measure the friction of other surfaces such as wood, carpet, plastic, glass, or other materials.

SHOW YOUR RESULTS:

Put numbers of paper clips in a data table like this for "Go Easy":

Material Tested	Block First Moved (Number of Paper Clips)	Block Moved Length of Board (Number of Paper Clips)
Cardboard		
Sandpaper		

Make a bar graph that compares your results. Explain the differences you see. For "Go," add rows to the data table for each kind of sandpaper you test and make bar graphs.

For "Go Far," make data tables for the surfaces and objects you test. Explain how the forces of inertia and friction vary with the surface.

Tips and Tricks

- Make sure the string is not under the block. It can get in the way and affect your results.
- You'll have a better project if you repeat each test several times and average your results.

Will a Ball Bounce Higher If It Is Dropped from a Greater Height?

TALK IT OVER:

What factors affect how high a ball bounces? Do some balls bounce higher than others? If you drop a ball from a high place, will it bounce higher than if you drop it from lower down? How can you find out?

GET:

- Board
- Yardstick (preferably marked in centimeters) or meterstick
- Tape

- Table
- Small, rubber ball
- A helper

 GO

1. Place the board on the floor under the edge of the table.

2. Stand the measuring stick vertically from the board to the table. Turn the numbers toward you, so you can see them. Put the 0 end on the board. Tape the stick to the table's edge, like this:

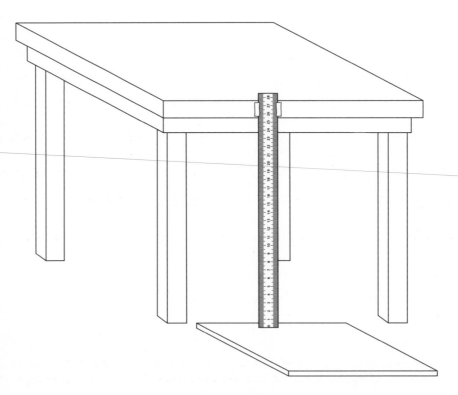

3. Lie down on the floor, looking at the measuring stick straight on, so you can see the numbers clearly. Ask your helper to hold the ball with its upper edge at the 20-cm. mark on the measuring stick. When you are ready, ask your helper to drop the ball. Watch carefully and note the high point of the ball's bounce *to the nearest centimeter,* like this:

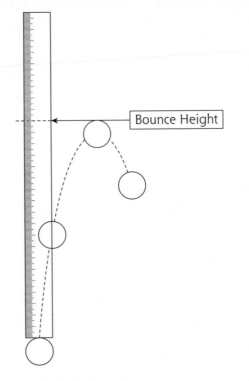

Note: You may need to practice this a few times so you are sure that you are seeing the number at the high point of the ball's bounce.

4. Record the height of the bounce. Repeat four times, so you have five trials. Find the average:

$$\frac{\text{Trial 1 + Trial 2 + Trial 3 + Trial 4 + Trial 5}}{5} = \text{average bounce height}$$

5. Repeat steps 3 and 4, dropping the ball from 40 cm, 60 cm, and 80 cm. Conduct five trials from each drop height and average your results.

STAY SAFE:
Watch out. Don't let that bouncing ball biff you in the nose!

GO EASY

Follow the "Go" procedure. Get an adult to help you record and average the numbers. If you have trouble seeing the centimeter numbers, you can work in inches. The numbers are bigger and the units farther apart.

FORCES AND MOTION

GO FAR

Compare different kinds of balls. Try to discover a "rule" that correctly predicts bounce height for all of them.

SHOW YOUR RESULTS:

Put bounce heights in a data table like this for "Go" and "Go Easy":

Drop Height	Trial 1	Trial 2	Trial 3	Trial 4	Trial 5	Average
20 cm						
40 cm						
60 cm . . . and so on						

For "Go Easy," make a bar graph of the average bounce height from the different drop heights. For "Go," make a line graph with drop height on the horizontal axis and bounce height on the vertical axis. Whichever graph you make, write a sentence that tells how you think drop height affects bounce height.

For "Go Far," make a line graph as for "Go," using different colored lines to compare the different balls you tested. Tell whether the "rule" you discovered applies to all the balls you tried.

Tips and Tricks

- Don't throw the ball. Just release it. Extra force will only push your ball sideways and make your bounce height harder to read.
- If you have a camera that can take stop-action pictures or multiple, continuous images, you may be able to take photographs to show both drop heights and bounce heights. Remember to set your camera on its fastest speed so it "stops" the ball in midair.

What Is the Tensile Strength of Fishing Line?

TALK IT OVER:

Printed on a package of fishing line is a *test number,* often in pounds and kilograms. It is supposed to mean that the line will hold that much weight, but probably not much more. How can you test the lines to see whether they perform as they should?

GET:

- 5-gallon bucket
- Kitchen scale or laboratory balance
- Several different weights of fishing line
- Scissors

- Metric ruler
- Metric measuring cup
- Water
- A tree limb and a place to work outdoors

GO

1. Using a kitchen scale, weigh the bucket. Record its weight.
2. Outdoors, tie a long piece of fishing line to the limb of a tree. Use the following knot. It will not slip.

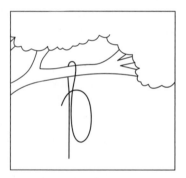

Step 1

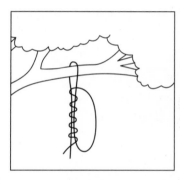

Step 2

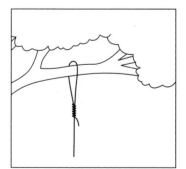

Step 3

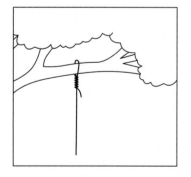

Step 4

3. Tie the other end of the line to the bail of the bucket, adjusting the length of the line so that the bucket hangs about 50 cm from the ground, like this:

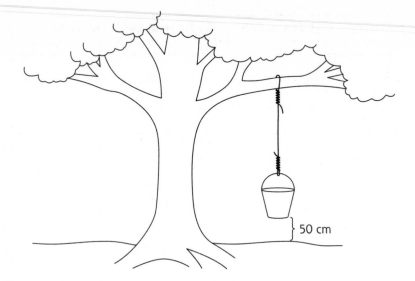

4. Measure 1 cup (250 milliliters) of water into the measuring cup. Pour the water into the bucket. Keep adding water in 250-ml amounts, keeping track of the number you add, until the line breaks. Stand back: Don't get splashed.

5. Calculate the total weight required to break the line. It is the weight of the bucket *plus* the weight of the water you added (the last addition before the break). The weight of the water is easily expressed in grams, because 1 ml weighs 1 gram. So you were adding weight 250 grams at a time.

STAY SAFE:
Don't have your hand or foot under the bucket when it breaks. It could hurt!

GO EASY
The "Go" procedure will work for you.

GO FAR
Tensile strength is the amount of force a material can withstand before it stretches, tears, or breaks. After you test fishing lines using the "Go" procedure, design and carry out your own experiment to test the tensile strength of something else. You might try carpet fibers, rope, threads, yarns, or human hairs.

SHOW YOUR RESULTS:

Put weights in a data table like this:

Package Label Test Weight of Line (in Grams)#	Weight Held before Breaking (in Grams; 1 ml water = 1 gram)ᵚ
454	
906	
1,360	

#To change kilograms to grams, multiply by 1,000.

ᵚDon't forget to add the weight of the bucket.

Make bar graphs comparing the advertised and actual tensile strength of the fishing lines. For "Go Far," make similar tables and graphs for any materials you test. For all experiments, display a drawing of your experimental setup.

Tips and Tricks

- Your experiment will take longer, but you'll get measurements that are more accurate if you add water in 100-ml increments.
- You'll get a more accurate weight for your bucket if you borrow a triple-beam balance from your school science lab.

How Does the Volume of Air Affect How Far a Balloon Rocket Travels?

TALK IT OVER:

A famous scientist once showed that "every action has an equal and opposite reaction." You can prove that by jumping off the front of a skateboard. Which way does the board travel? Backward . . . and with a force that equals your weight! The same principle propels rockets. How can you show the effect of force on the distance a rocket travels?

GET: _____

- A large, outdoor space with 2 poles, trees, or fence posts that are 5 or more meters apart
- Scissors
- Fishing line, 5 meters or more in length
- Flexible, metal measuring tape (the kind carpenters use), 5 meters or longer
- Fabric measuring tape (the kind people who sew use), marked in centimeters
- Masking tape
- Round balloon
- A helper (It takes more than two hands to do this experiment!)
- Plastic straw

GO

1. Find a spot outdoors where you can work. You need two trees, poles, or posts that are 5 or more meters apart. Measure the distance between the supports with your metal tape, like this:

2. Tie one end of the fishing line to one of the supports, 1 meter off the ground. Stretch the fishing line to the other support, but do not tie it. Cut the line, leaving about 50 cm extra.

3. On the second support, measure up 1 meter from the ground. Place a piece of masking tape at that height. It will serve as your starting point, like this:

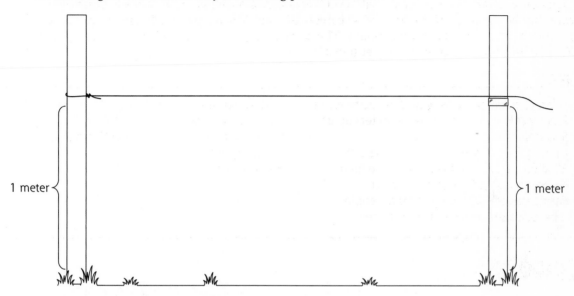

1 meter   1 meter

4. Have your helper blow up the balloon *slightly*. Do not tie the balloon. While your helper holds the balloon shut so no air escapes, measure the distance around the balloon at its widest point. Use the sewing measuring tape, like this:

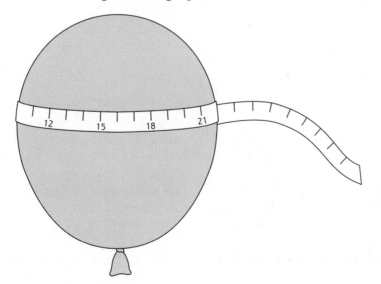

FORCES AND MOTION

5. Record that number, which is the circumference of the balloon.

6. While your helper continues to hold the balloon, attach a straw to the balloon with tape, like this:

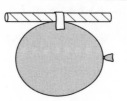

7. Your helper is still holding. (Helpers need patience and dedication.) Thread the fishing line through the straw. Raise the line to the starting point on the support. Pull the line taut and position the balloon on the line, like this:

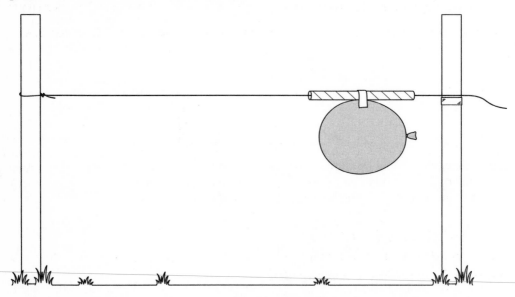

8. When you say go, your helper will release the balloon, and your model rocket will fly along the fishing line.

9. While you continue to hold the line, have your helper run out and put a finger on the line at the point where the rocket stops. Use your flexible metal tape to measure the distance that your rocket travels in centimeters.

10. Repeat this many more times, each time adding a little more air to the balloon. (The more air in your balloon, the greater its circumference.)

STAY SAFE:

Don't stand in front of the balloon when you launch it. It could smack you a wallop.

GO EASY

The "Go" procedure will work for you. Get an adult's help with the setup, measuring, and data collection.

GO FAR

Use volume, not circumference, in your data tables. Although circumference is *proportional* to the volume of air in the balloon, we did not actually measure volume in the "Go" procedure. (Volume is the total amount of space an object fills.) You can, however, calculate the balloon's volume from its circumference (assuming that the balloon is a sphere, which it isn't, but it is close) in two steps:

1. Find the radius, which is the distance from the center of the sphere to its outer edge:

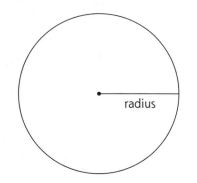

radius = circumference ÷ 6.28

2. Use the radius to find the volume.

volume = 4.18 × radius × radius × radius

For example, if the circumference of your balloon is 21 cm, its radius is 21 ÷ 6.28 = 3.34 cm. Its volume is 4.18 × 3.34 cm × 3.34 cm × 3.34 cm = 156 cm³.

You may also want to add time and speed to your experiment. Use a stopwatch (more helpers' hands are needed) to measure the time of your balloon's flight. Divide distance by time to obtain speed. Compare speed to the balloon's volume. What is the relationship?

SHOW YOUR RESULTS:

Put your data in a table like this for "Go" and "Go Easy":

Circumference	Distance Traveled

Make a line graph that relates distance traveled on the vertical axis to the circumference of the balloon on the horizontal axis.

For "Go Far," use a table like this:

Circumference	Volume#	Distance Traveled	Time	Speed#

#Calculated values

For "Go Far," make separate line graphs that relate distance and speed to volume.

For all procedures, write your conclusions in a few sentences. State how the amount of air in the balloon affected how far or how fast your model rocket traveled.

Tips and Tricks

Align the straw straight with the long axis of the balloon. If you don't, some of the force will push the balloon sideways—not straight down the fishing line—and you won't get good measurements of distance or speed. Like this:

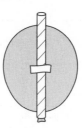

Not like this:

Not like this:

What Makes a Pendulum Swing Fast or Slow?

TALK IT OVER:

If you've ever looked at a grandfather clock, you've seen a pendulum swinging inside. A pendulum is just a weight suspended from above by a bar or string. In the clock, the steady swing of the pendulum measures time. What determines whether a pendulum swings fast or slow?

GET: _____

- Ruler
- Scissors
- String
- Felt-tip marker

- 1 large metal washer (You'll need more than 1 for "Go Far.")
- Tape
- A clock with a second hand or a stopwatch

 GO

1. Cut a piece of string 60 cm (about 24 inches) long. Tie the washer to the end of the string, like this:

2. Using the ruler, measure from the knot (not the loose end) along the string. Make a mark with the felt-tip marker every 10 centimeters (4 inches), like this:

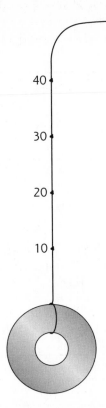

3. Tape the string to the table so that the washer hangs down and the distance from the table's edge to the knot is 10 cm (4 in), like this:

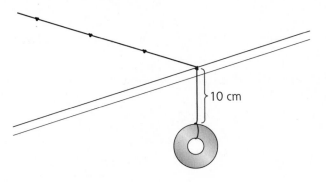

10 cm

4. Pull the washer to one side, in line with the table's edge. Let go. Make sure your pendulum swings freely and doesn't hit anything.

5. Now get ready to use your clock or stopwatch. You will pull the washer back and let go. Count how many times your pendulum swings in 15 seconds. Record that number.

6. Reposition the pendulum so that the distance from the table's edge to the washer is 20 cm (8 in). Then repeat steps 4 and 5.

7. Retest at lengths of 30, 40, and 50 cm (12, 16, and 20 inches).

STAY SAFE:

Watch where you swing the pendulum. Don't swing it into anyone's face.

GO EASY

The "Go" procedure will work for you. Get an adult's help with timing, counting, and recording.

GO FAR

Experiment to find out whether the amount of weight on the string, the height of the release, or some other factor affects how fast the pendulum swings. Then make pendulums that swing at known rates. Use them as clocks that can measure 1 minute's time accurately.

SHOW YOUR RESULTS:

For "Go" and "Go Easy," record the number of swings in a table like this:

Pendulum length	Number of Swings in 15 Seconds
10 cm	
20 cm	
30 cm . . . and so on	

Make line or bar graphs that relate the number of swings (on the vertical axis) to the string length (on the horizontal axis).

For "Go Far," design similar tables to match whatever experiments you conduct. Make bar or line graphs that will show whether the factors you studied actually make a difference in the rate of a pendulum's swing.

For all the experiments, write a statement that says, "The _____ (factor I studied) does/does not affect the rate of pendulum swing. I know this because _____."

Tips and Tricks

You can count the movement of the pendulum from one side to the other as 1 swing, like this:

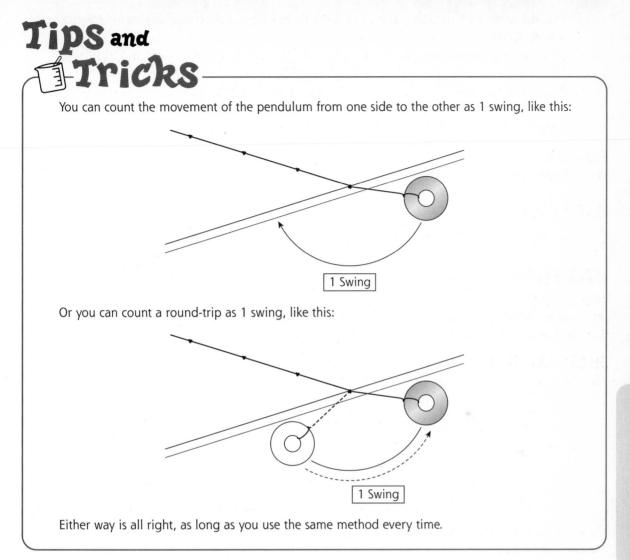

1 Swing

Or you can count a round-trip as 1 swing, like this:

1 Swing

Either way is all right, as long as you use the same method every time.

Do Some Liquids Heat Faster than Others?

TALK IT OVER:

How do you make things hotter? What is heat? How do you measure heat? Are some liquids easier to heat than others?

GET: _____

- Water (at room temperature)
- Jar
- Glass measuring cup, microwave safe
- Vegetable oil (at room temperature)

- Hot pad
- Digital instant-read thermometer*
- Access to a microwave oven

GO

1. The night before you start your experiment, set a jar of water and a container of oil on the countertop. By morning, they will be the same (room) temperature.

2. Measure ½ cup of water in the measuring cup. Measure and record the temperature.

3. Place the cup and water in the microwave. Heat at full power for 15 seconds. Measure and record the temperature of the water.

4. Repeat step 3 another seven times, recording temperatures for a total of 2 minutes of heating.

5. Clean and dry the measuring cup. Repeat steps 2–4 using oil.

STAY SAFE:

Avoid burns and spills. Get an adult's help in handling the hot cups and liquids.

GO EASY

Follow the "Go" procedure, but make measurements every 30 seconds instead of every 15.

GO FAR

Specific heat is the amount of heat required to raise the temperature of 1 gram of a substance 1°C. Modify the "Go" procedure so you can calculate the specific heats of water and oil. (*Hint:* You will need to know the output of your microwave.) You might compare molasses, corn syrup, vinegar, and varieties of oil including corn and canola. Also, try comparing solutions such as sugar or salt water made in different concentrations (such as ¼, ½, ¾, and 1 teaspoon sugar or salt per ½ cup of water).

SHOW YOUR RESULTS:

Record temperatures in a data table like this for "Go Easy":

Time	Temperature of Water	Temperature of Oil
0 seconds (before heating)		
30 seconds		
1 minute		
1 minute 30 seconds		
2 minutes		

Make a bar graph that compares the two liquids.

For "Go," use the same kind of data table, but record temperatures in 15-second intervals. Make a line graph of temperature (on the vertical axis) by time (on the horizontal axis), using different colors of lines to compare water and oil.

For "Go Far," make data tables and line graphs that compare the specific heat values you determined. Look up published tables of specific heat values and see how your results compare.

HEAT

Tips and Tricks

Don't use a digital thermometer from the health section of your pharmacy or discount store. It is meant for taking human body temperatures, so its range is too narrow for this experiment. Choose a thermometer from the kitchen aids department. It will measure the wide range of temperatures you need.

Many thermometers read temperatures in both Fahrenheit (°F) and Celsius (°C). You can use either for this experiment; just be careful not to confuse them. If you want to work as scientists do, use °C.

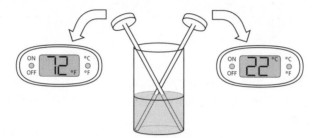

Keep the tip of the thermometer in the liquid. If it touches the container, you won't get an accurate reading. Like this:

Not like this:

This is a good experiment to repeat several times. Averages of your temperatures from multiple trials are better than the results of a single trial.

Will Some Colors Keep You Cooler than Others?

TALK IT OVER:

Which keeps you cooler on a hot day, a black shirt or a white shirt? What about other colors? How can you find out?

GET: _____

- Black and white construction paper
- Ruler
- Scissors
- Tape

- 2 digital instant-read thermometers*
- Sunny spot or gooseneck desk lamp
- Clock or timer
- Other colors of construction paper to test

GO

1. Cut pieces of black and white construction paper that measure approximately 10 cm x 20 cm (4" x 8"). Fold in half along the length and tape the sides. You have made pockets that the thermometers can fit in.

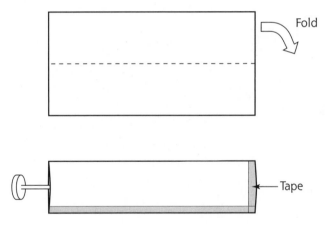

Fold

Tape

2. Put the thermometers in the pockets. Turn them on and read the beginning temperature. They should read the same. Turn them off to save battery power.

3. Place the thermometers in a sunny place or under a gooseneck desk lamp. After 10 minutes and without moving the thermometers, turn them on and read the temperatures. Turn them off.

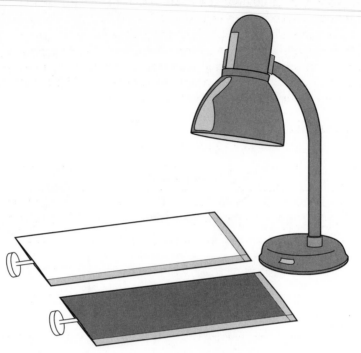

4. Take additional temperature readings every 10 minutes for 1 hour.
5. Repeat steps 1–4 with other colors you would like to test.

STAY SAFE:

Be careful with a desk lamp. A hot bulb can burn your fingers!

GO EASY

Follow the "Go" procedure, but read the temperature only twice: once before you begin and again after 1 hour. Use subtraction to find out which temperature changed most. Try to explain why.

GO FAR

The heat absorption properties of colored materials depend on many factors, including how much light is reflected and what wavelengths of light (colors) are absorbed. Use the "Go" procedure to test different materials of the same color. Also, you might approach the question a different way. Try to find which colors and materials work best as insulation, reducing heat loss. Make some telephone calls to see whether you can borrow a *pyranometer* from a commercial or college laboratory. A pyranometer allows you to measure *albedo,* the amount of light reflected from a surface. Perhaps you can find a way to relate albedo differences to your heat data.

SHOW YOUR RESULTS:

Record temperatures in a data table like this for "Go":

Temperature								
Color Tested	**0 Mins**	**10 Mins**	**20 Mins**	**30 Mins**	**40 Mins**	**50 Mins**	**60 Mins**	**Change (60 Mins – Starting Temperature)**
Black								
White								
Red . . . and so on								

Make a line graph that shows how temperature changed over time. Use different colored lines on the graph to represent the colors of the papers you tested.

For "Go Easy," put your data in a table like this:

Color Tested	Starting Temperature	Temperature after 1 Hour	Difference
Black			
White			

Make a bar graph of your data. Write a sentence that describes and explains any differences.

For "Go Far," make data tables and line graphs as for "Go." Try to explain the differences you find in the heat absorption or insulating abilities of materials of the same color. If you measure albedo, try to answer the following question: Do materials with greater albedo absorb more or less heat?

HEAT

Tips and Tricks

- If you use a gooseneck lamp, the bulb should be at least 100 watts. Bend the neck of the lamp so that the bulb is close above the thermometers. Make sure its light falls evenly on both.
- Many thermometers read temperatures in both Fahrenheit (°F) and Celsius (°C). You can use either for this experiment; just be careful not to confuse them. If you want to work as scientists do, use °C.
- You'll get better results if you conduct several trials and average your data.

Which Metal Conducts Heat Best?

TALK IT OVER:

What is heat? How can you tell when something is hot? If you leave a metal spoon in a hot drink, how does it feel? Does heat travel through metals? Do some metals conduct heat better than others do?

GET:

- Pitcher
- Refrigerator
- Water
- Metal rods, 1/16-inch diameter, 12 inches long: 3 each copper, steel, and brass or other metals of your choice*

- 8 juice glasses
- Kettle to boil water in
- Hot pad
- Digital instant-read thermometer*

GO

1. Put a pitcher of water in the refrigerator and leave it overnight, so it gets very cold.

2. Bend each of the metal rods in half, then in half again to make nine upside-down "U" shapes, like this:

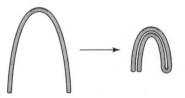

These are the metal bridges you will use in step 5. Make three bridges from each of the three metals.

3. Arrange the juice glasses in pairs, close together but not touching.

4. Ask an adult to boil some water for you. Ask your adult helper to fill four of the juice glasses—one glass in each pair—with the boiling water. Fill the other four glasses—the other glass in each pair—with the cold water from the pitcher. You now have four pairs of glasses—one with hot water and one with cold water in each pair.

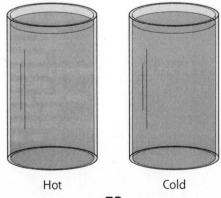

Hot   Cold

73

5. Work quickly. Use the instant read, digital thermometer to measure the temperature of the water in each glass of cold water. Record.

6. Between the first pair of glasses, put the 3 copper bridges. Between the second pair, put the 3 steel bridges. Between the third pair, put the 3 brass bridges. Leave the last set of glasses without any bridges. Make sure the metal bridges are beneath the water level in both glasses. Your setup should look like this:

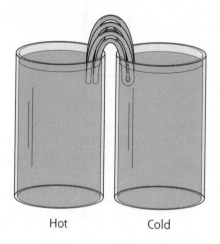

Hot   Cold

7. Every 5 minutes for 30 minutes, take and record the temperature in each glass of cold water. Calculate the total change in the water's temperature by subtracting the beginning temperature from the ending temperature:

ending temperature – beginning temperature = change in temperature in 30 minutes

STAY SAFE:

Be careful with the metal rods. Their cut ends can be sharp. Have an adult boil and pour the hot water for you. Be careful not to spill the hot water. It can burn you.

GO EASY

Measure the temperature of the cold water at 0 minutes (when you start) and again after 30 minutes only.

GO FAR

Are metals that are good conductors of heat also good conductors of electricity? Design and perform an experiment to find out. You'll find some procedures that may help you in the chapter on electricity.

SHOW YOUR RESULTS:

For "Go," make a data table like this:

Temperature of Cold Water								
Metal Bridge	**0 Mins**	**5 Mins**	**10 Mins**	**15 Mins**	**20 Mins**	**25 Mins**	**30 Mins**	**Change in Temperature**
None (control)								
Copper								
Steel								
Brass								

Make a line graph that compares the temperature changes you obtained with the different metal bridges you tested. Use different colors of lines to represent the metals. Put a line on the graph for the "control," which had no bridges. Tell which metal conducts heat best and tell how your data support the conclusion you draw.

For "Go Easy," use only the 0 minutes, 30 minutes, and change in temperature columns of the data table. Make a bar graph with the kind of bridge (including the control) on the horizontal axis and the change in temperature after 30 minutes on the vertical axis. Use your graph to say which metal you think conducted heat best and why you think so.

For "Go Far," expand your project to include your experimental design and data for investigating the electrical conductivity of metals. Draw a conclusion that relates conduction of both heat and electricity.

Tips and Tricks

- This experimental design allows some heat loss to the air. The *difference* between your bridge data and the control data is a good measure of the conductivity of each metal. The greater the difference, the better conductor of heat the metal is.
- Although scientists usually use Celsius (°C) in their experiments, you'll be better able to see differences in this experiment if you use the Fahrenheit (°F) scale.
- Don't let the thermometer touch the metal bridges or the sides of the glasses. You won't get accurate temperature readings.
- If you can't find metal rods, substitute heavy gauge wires made of different metals. You can buy them in hardware and craft stores or order them from a jewelry-making catalog.

HEAT

Do Some Colors of M&Ms Melt Faster than Others?

TALK IT OVER:

M&M candies advertise that they "melt in your mouth, not in your hand." What do you think that means? Do M&Ms ever melt before you can eat them? Do you think some colors of M&Ms melt at a lower temperature than others? How can you find out?

GET:

- White paper (not Styrofoam) plates
- Jar lid
- Pencil
- Package of M&M candies, plain (not peanut)
- School glue
- Access to a microwave oven

GO

1. Center the jar lid on a paper plate. Draw around it with a pencil. Make a plate with a circle for each color of M&M candy you want to test.

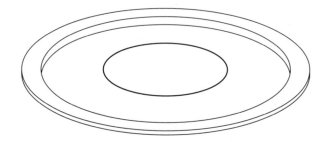

2. Open the package of candies and divide the colors. For each color, you will need 5 candies to test.

3. Put 5 tiny drops of school glue at equal distances around the pencil circle. Put 5 candies of a single color—with the M down—on 1 plate, 1 on each drop of glue. Make the same kind of plate for each color you want to test. Let the glue dry before going on. Your plates should look like this:

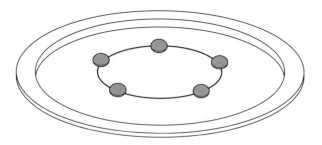

4. Microwave each plate, one at a time, on full power, in 20-second increments. Look for cracks. Record the total number of candies that are cracked at each time interval. Also record other observations in as much detail as you can.

STAY SAFE:

Don't touch the candies. They can get very hot! Also, do not eat the candies you experiment with.

GO EASY

Follow the "Go" procedure, but use only yellow and one other color.

GO FAR

Follow the "Go," procedure with all the colors. Then repeat the experiment with peanut M&Ms. Is there a difference?

SHOW YOUR RESULTS:

Use a data table like this for "Go":

Color of Candy	Number of Cracked Candies						
	0 Sec	20 Sec	40 Sec	60 Sec	80 Sec	100 Sec	120 Sec
Yellow	0						
Observations							
Green	0						
Observations							
Red	0						
Observations . . . and so on							

Make a line graph showing the number of cracked candies at each time interval. Use a different color line for each color of candy. Display your plates along with your observations so people can see differences for themselves.

For "Go Easy," use the same kind of data table as for "Go," but use fewer rows. Make a bar graph that compares the time required to crack all 5 candies. State in a single sentence a conclusion supported by your data.

For "Go Far," make data tables and line graphs for each color and kind of candy you test. Draw conclusions and give reasons for them.

HEAT

How Does the Sun's Direction Affect Temperature?

TALK IT OVER:

Where does the sun appear to be in the sky at different times of the day? Does the sun feel hotter or cooler when you face in different directions? How can you find out?

GET:

- Half-gallon milk carton
- Sand or stones
- 4 indoor-outdoor tube thermometers*
- Tape
- Plastic wrap
- Compass
- Sunny spot outdoors

GO

1. Start this experiment in the morning on a sunny day. Put sand or stones in the milk carton to keep it from blowing over in a breeze.

2. Tape 4 thermometers to the milk carton, one on each side, like this:

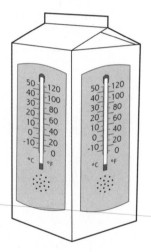

3. Wrap the carton and thermometers in plastic wrap.

4. Find a sunny spot outside that will not be in the shade at any time during the day. Using the compass, find which direction is north. Note where south, east, and west are.

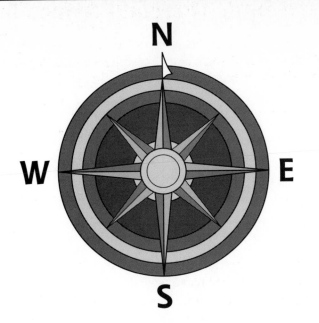

5. Set the milk cartons so that the thermometers face the four directions exactly, like this:

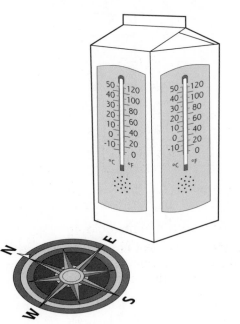

6. Look at the milk carton's shadow. It tells you that the sun is in the *opposite* direction in the sky. (For example, if the shadow is falling toward the west, the sun is in the eastern sky.) Record this direction.

7. Wait about 20 minutes. Then take your first temperature readings, one from each thermometer (direction). Record.

8. Every hour throughout the day, read and record the four temperatures again.

HEAT

STAY SAFE:

Never look into the sun. It can blind you. *Infer* where the sun is in the sky from the shadow the milk carton casts.

GO EASY

Use the "Go" procedure, but read temperatures only three times: once in the early morning, once around noon, and once in late afternoon. Get an adult's help with reading the compass and the thermometers.

GO FAR

The results of this experiment help explain both seasonal differences and climate regions on planet Earth. Do some research in your library and on the Internet to use in your project display.

SHOW YOUR RESULTS:

Record temperatures and the sun's direction in a table like this, using only three time columns for "Go Easy":

Direction	Temperature					
	9:00 a.m.	10:00 a.m.	11:00 a. m.	12:00 noon	1:00 p.m.	2:00 p.m. . . . and so on
North						
East						
South						
West						
Sun's direction						

For "Go Easy," make three bar graphs that show the temperature in each direction at three times of the day. Use the direction of shadows and your temperature data to answer the following question: Where is the sun in the sky at different times of the day?

For "Go," make a line graph of temperature (on the vertical axis) by time of day (on the horizontal axis). Use four different colors of lines to represent the four directions. State conclusions that relate your temperature data to the position of the sun in the sky.

For "Go Far," add information on seasons and Earth's climatic regions. Relate both to your data on temperature and direction.

Tips and Tricks

- Make sure to wrap your experiment in plastic wrap. You'll get bigger temperature differences. Can you explain why?
- Look carefully at your compass and the shadow cast by the milk carton. Read the *opposite* compass direction as accurately as you can. For example, if the shadow lies to the NNE (north northeast), the sun's direction is SSW (south southwest).

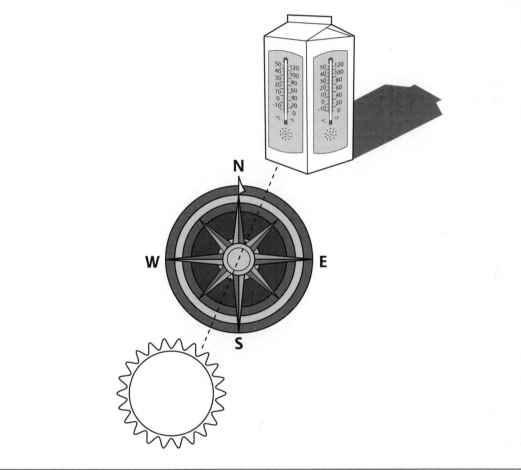

How Does Light Make Colors?

TALK IT OVER:

What color is light? What is a rainbow? Why do objects look different colors? How can we find out about different colors of light?

GET:

- Cellophane*: red, blue, and green
- Scissors
- 3 strong flashlights
- Tape
- White paper
- Dark room
- Colored pencils or markers
- Cellophane in other colors

GO

1. Cut pieces of red, blue, and green cellophane big enough to cover the lights of the three flashlights. Tape the pieces in place—one color per flashlight.

2. In a dark room, shine each of your lights on a white piece of paper. If the color looks too pale or the light beam too white, tape on another layer or two of cellophane. (Your goal is a brightly colored light, and cellophanes vary in their thickness and color intensity.)

3. In a dark room, shine the three colors of light on the white paper so that they overlap, like this:

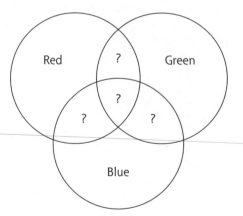

4. Study the overlap areas carefully. Try holding the flashlights closer to the paper and then farther away. The overlap areas may be easier to observe if you back off.

5. Make and color a drawing to record what you see. Be sure to show the individual colors plus what you see in all four areas of overlap. (**Hint:** The overlap areas are blue/red, red/green; green/blue, and blue/red/green.)

6. Repeat the experiment with any other colors you want to test.

STAY SAFE:

Stumbling around in dark rooms can be dangerous. Be sure to set up your experiment before you turn off the lights.

GO EASY

The "Go" procedure will work for you.

GO FAR

Natural light is white, but it contains all the colors. A prism breaks white light into its colors. You see those colors in a rainbow. Red objects look red because they absorb all the colors except red. They *reflect* (bounce) red light back to your eyes. In the same way, blue objects look blue because they absorb all the colors *except* blue. However, objects look their true color only in white light. Shine different colors of light on them, and their color changes. You can investigate how this works by shining colored lights on colored objects in a dark room and recording the colors they appear to be. Try to discover a rule that accurately predicts how the color of light and the color of an object interact.

SHOW YOUR RESULTS:

For "Go" and "Go Easy," display the diagrams that show your results. Write a few sentences to describe and explain what you observed.

For "Go Far," display—along with your drawings—some of the objects and colors of light you investigated. Report your observations and any "rule" you devised to explain them.

Tips and Tricks

- Juggling three flashlights at once can be tricky. Get a friend to help you hold the flashlights in the right places.

- Expand your project. Cut pieces of red, blue, and yellow translucent plastic* from the backs of report covers. Without looking at the sun, place the pieces on a bright window and move them around. Can you make the colors of the rainbow? Try to figure out why these results differ from what you observed with colored light.

Does Ultraviolet (UV) Light Pass through Some Colors More than Others?

TALK IT OVER:

Light travels in waves. The waves have different lengths called (no surprises here!) *wavelengths*. Different colors of light have different wavelengths. Red light, for example, has a longer wavelength than blue light. Ultraviolet (UV) light has a wavelength so short, we can't see it.

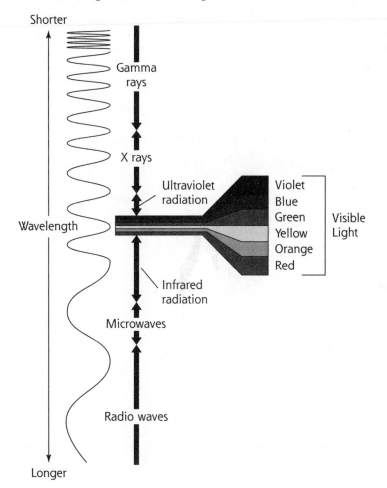

GET:

- 4 small juice glasses
- Measuring cup
- Water
- Red and blue food coloring
- Towel
- 4 pieces of Sunprint paper*

- Tray
- Ballpoint pen
- Sunny spot outdoors
- Access to a black-and-white photocopy machine
- Your grayscale (See "How to Make a Grayscale" in Part III.)

GO

1. Work indoors, away from bright light. Put ¼ cup of water in each of the juice glasses.
2. To the first glass, add 2 drops of blue food coloring. To the second, add 2 drops of red. To the third, add 1 drop of red and 1 drop of blue to make purple. Add no color to the water in the fourth glass.
3. Swirl the water in the first three glasses to mix the food coloring thoroughly. Careful. Don't spill.
4. Make sure the bottoms of all three glasses are dry. If they aren't, dry them with a towel.
5. Place 4 pieces of Sunprint paper on the tray, blue side up. With the ballpoint pen, label the pieces in small letters in a corner: "blue," "red," "purple," and "clear."

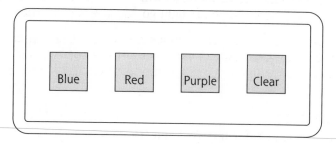

6. Set the glasses on the paper. Match the color of the water to the label you wrote on the paper.

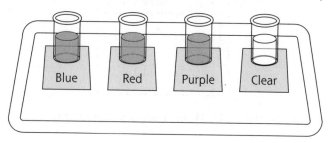

7. Carefully carry the tray out to a sunny spot. Don't spill. Turn the tray so that shadows don't fall on any of the papers.

8. Leave in the sun until the papers turn white—between 1 and 5 minutes. Take the papers indoors to a sink and rinse them in water for 1 minute.

9. Allow the papers to dry completely before you go on.

10. Place the papers on the black-and-white photocopier and make a copy. Compare the spots on the papers to your grayscale. From your grayscale, pick the number of the gray value that best describes the spot on your Sunprint paper.

STAY SAFE:

Nothing in this experiment can hurt you, but be careful with food coloring. It can stain your skin and clothes.

GO EASY

The "Go" procedure will work for you.

GO FAR

This experiment works because ultraviolet light from the sun changes Sunprint paper from blue to white. Then the water reacts with the paper, causing the white (exposed to UV) areas to turn dark blue. Where UV is totally blocked, the paper turns white. Partial exposure to UV results in a shade of blue. The darker the blue, the more ultraviolet light got through to the paper.

You can expand this experiment by making solutions and testing other colors. Try green, yellow, and colors you mix, such as orange. Also, experiment to see whether the intensity of the color makes a difference. Compare the gray values of the spots that appear beneath solutions made with 1, 2, 3, and 4 drops of a single color.

SHOW YOUR RESULTS:

Put gray values in a data table like this for "Go" and "Go Easy":

Color	Gray value
Red	
Blue	
Purple	

For "Go Far," add other colors to the table. Make a separate table to compare different intensities of a single color.

For all projects, display your Sunprints and your photocopies. Make a bar graph showing how the gray values of the spots compare. State a brief conclusion and try to explain any differences you see.

Do Some Sunglasses Block UV Light Better than Others?

TALK IT OVER:

You can't see ultraviolet (UV) light. Its wavelengths are shorter than the light you see. But it can hurt your eyes. Sunglasses prevent ultraviolet from getting to your eyes. Do some sunglasses block UV light better than others?

Note: Do *not* use good sunglasses that you want to keep for this project. Removing the lenses from the frames will bend the sunglasses beyond repair.

GET:

- Pliers
- Inexpensive or recycled sunglasses or glasses with tinted lenses
- Old pair of glasses with untinted lenses
- Transparent tape
- Pen or marker
- Glass cleaner and cloth

- Tray
- Sunprint paper*, 1 piece for each lens you test
- Sunny spot
- Water
- Access to a black-and-white photocopier
- Your grayscale (See "How to Make a Grayscale" in Part III.)

GO

1. Work indoors, out of sunlight. Ask an adult to use pliers to bend the frames on the glasses and remove one of the lenses from each pair you want to test.

2. Put a piece of transparent tape on a corner of each lens. Bend the tape back onto itself so no sticky sides are exposed. Write a number on the tape—a different number for each lens you want to test.

3. Clean each lens with glass cleaner and a clean cloth.

4. Place sheets of Sunprint paper on the tray—one for each lens you want to test. Put a number in the corner of each sheet to match the number tags you put on the lenses. Put each lens with the curved side down on its labeled paper.

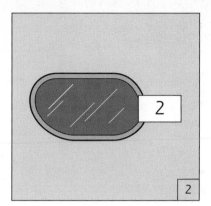

5. Carefully carry the tray outdoors to a sunny spot. Make sure all the sheets are fully exposed to sunlight. No shadows anywhere!

6. Leave in the sun until the papers turn white—between 1 and 5 minutes. Take the papers indoors to a sink and rinse them in water for 1 minute.

7. Allow the papers to dry completely before you go on.

8. Place the papers on the black-and-white photocopier and make a copy. Compare the spots on the papers to your grayscale. From your grayscale, pick the number of the gray value that best describes the spot on your Sunprint paper.

STAY SAFE:

Handle lens and broken frames carefully. Sharp edges can cut you.

GO EASY

The "Go" procedure will work for you.

GO FAR

Ultraviolet light changes chemicals in Sunprint paper. It changes the paper from blue to white. Then the water reacts with the changed chemicals in the paper, causing the white (exposed) areas to turn dark blue. Where UV was totally blocked, the paper turns white. Partial exposure to UV results in a shade of blue. The darker the blue, the more UV got through a *translucent* object, such as a lens. Try to relate your observations to the UV information given (sometimes) on the labels attached to sunglasses.

You might like to extend your investigation using a UV intensity meter and lens tester card*. Follow the directions on the card to measure UV levels in sunlight and the blocking ability of your lenses.

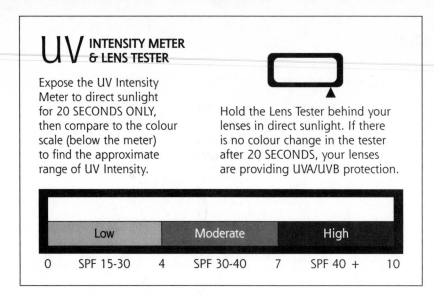

Another project might be a comparison of sunscreen creams and lotions. Smear small amounts of sunscreens with different SPF values on clear plastic. (SPF stands for sun protection factor. The higher the factor number, the greater the UV protection is supposed to be.) Place the smeared sheets over Sunprint paper and proceed as you did in "Go." Do the sunscreens live up to their advertising?

SHOW YOUR RESULTS:

Put gray values in a data table like this for "Go" and "Go Easy":

Lens Number	Gray Value
1	
2	
3 . . . and so on	

For "Go Far," make a similar table for the sunscreens you test, adding a column for the SPF on the product's label.

For all projects, display your Sunprints and your photocopies. Make a bar graph showing how the gray values of the spots compare. State brief conclusions and try to explain any differences you see.

Tips and Tricks

- You may need to adjust the light-dark setting on the photocopier until you get a good image that shows shades of gray clearly.
- Interpreting Sunprints can get confusing. Remember, the *darker* the spot, the *more* UV that got to it. A lighter spot (a lower gray value) means *less* UV reached the paper.

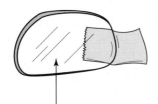

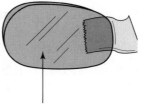

This lens let only a little UV through.

This lens let a lot of UV through.

How Many Images Can You Make with Mirrors?

TALK IT OVER:

Why do you see a reflection in a mirror? Is it possible to see more than one? How many might you make?

GET:

- 2 4" x 5" plastic mirrors* (3 for "Go Far")
- Plastic packing tape
- Protractor
- Ruler
- Pen

- Graph paper, 6 pieces
- Modeling clay
- Coin
- Camera or drawing materials

1. Stand the mirrors vertically and tape them together along their long edges so they are hinged, like this:

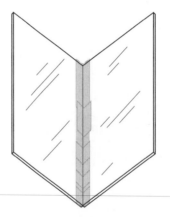

2. Move your hinge back and forth a few times. It should hold, but still allow the mirrors to move freely in all directions.

3. On separate pieces of graph paper, use your protractor to mark angles of 30°, 36°, 45°, 60°, 90°, and 180°. If you don't know how to do this, get an adult to help you.

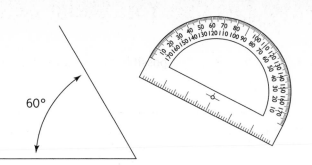

4. On each piece of graph paper, find a spot in the center, between the two angle lines, and 8 cm (about 3 inches) out from the point of the angle. Mark that spot.

5. Test your angles one at a time. Put the modeling clay at the center point you marked. Set the coin upright in the clay. Position your hinged mirrors on the angle lines you drew, like this:

6. Take a photograph or make a drawing to record what you see. Also record the number of coin images in a data table.

STAY SAFE:

Don't use glass mirrors. Their edges can be sharp.

GO EASY

Try only the 180°, 90°, and 60° angles.

GO FAR

This experiment works because light bounces off mirrors at predictable angles. If the bounced light hits another mirror, it bounces again, also at a predictable angle. It can do this several times before it reaches your eye, depending on the angle between the mirrors. A mathematic rule predicts how many images are visible. See whether you can discover it.

Expand your experiment by setting your hinged mirrors on a third mirror. See how many images you can count at the triple intersection.

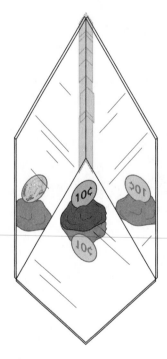

Plastic mirrors are available in many shapes and sizes, including convex, concave, and dome. Design experiments that will let you assess the numbers and forms of the images you obtain with them.

SHOW YOUR RESULTS:

Record the number of images you see in a table like this for "Go Easy":

Angle (in Degrees)	Number of Images
180	
90	
60	

Make a bar graph that shows the number of images (on the vertical axis) by the angles you tried (on the horizontal axis).

For "Go," add smaller angles to your data table and your bar graph. State the mathematical rule that relates angle to the number of images. For "Go Far," design data tables and graphs to match the experiments you conduct.

For all projects, display your photographs or drawings along with any conclusions you drew from your data. Display your materials along with your project so others can try some experiments for themselves.

Tips and 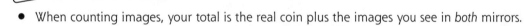 *Tricks*

- When counting images, your total is the real coin plus the images you see in *both* mirrors.
- Turn the coin so that heads faces one mirror and tails faces the other. Then look at the images. What do you notice about them? Report this observation as part of your project.

How Does Distance Affect the Spreading of Light?

TALK IT OVER:

If an object is close to a light, how does it look? How does it look if it is farther away? What happens to light as it travels across a distance? How can you find out?

GET: _____

- Peel-and-stick foam or felt, black, small sheet*
- Scissors
- Hole punch
- Bright flashlight
- Dim room
- Tape
- 1 sheet of graph paper, ¼-inch grid
- Tape measure
- Pencil
- Helper

 GO

1. Cut a small piece of peel-and-stick foam or felt a little larger than the beam end of the flashlight.
2. With the hole punch, punch a small, round hole in the foam or felt.
3. Peel off the back of the foam or felt and stick the piece to the flashlight. Make sure that you cover the edges and that no light leaks out around the sides when you turn the flashlight on.

4. In a dim room, tape the graph paper to the wall at a height you can see easily.
5. Have your helper stand very close to the graph paper and turn on the flashlight. Point the beam straight at the graph paper. Your helper has to stay very still while you perform steps 6 and 7.

6. With the tape measure, measure the distance from the paper to the flashlight. Record.

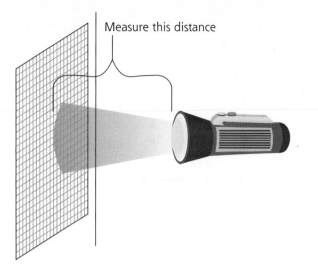

Measure this distance

7. With a pencil, draw a circle around the spot of light on the graph paper. Label it with the distance you measured in step 6. It should look something like this:

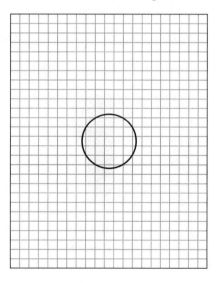

8. Now have your helper back up 1 or 2 centimeters (less than an inch) and repeat step 5 while you repeat steps 6 and 7.

9. Keep repeating these steps until you have a number of circles drawn on the graph paper and your biggest spot nearly fills the paper.

10. Count the number of squares contained within each circle. If half or more of a square is inside the circle, count it as 1. If less than half of a square is inside the circle, do not count it. Once a square is counted, it counts for all the circles that surround it. For example:

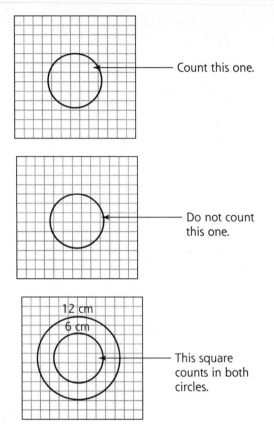

Count this one.

Do not count this one.

12 cm

6 cm

This square counts in both circles.

STAY SAFE:

Don't leave the flashlight on too long. The glass under the foam or felt can get hot.

GO EASY

Perform the "Go" procedure at three distances you measure. Try to get spots that are small, medium, and large.

GO FAR

The "Go" procedure works because light rays spread over a greater area as they travel. The spread also changes the intensity of light. Try to borrow a light meter from a photographer or your school's science lab. Design and carry out an experiment to measure the change in light intensity per unit of increased distance.

SHOW YOUR RESULTS:

Put the number of illuminated squares in a data table like this for "Go Easy" and "Go":

Distance	Lighted Area (in squares)
1 cm	
3 cm	
5 cm . . . and so on	

Make line graphs with distance on the horizontal axis and lighted area (in squares) on the vertical axis. The line that connects the points should suggest a conclusion you can write about the relationship between distance and lighted area.

For "Go Far," design a similar table and graph that will reveal how light intensity varies with distance.

Tips and Tricks

- If you don't have peel-and-stick foam or felt, punch a hole in black construction paper. Secure it to the flashlight with black electrical tape.
- Sometimes, reflections inside the flashlight's head cast secondary light patterns onto your graph paper. They are odd-shaped and irregular. Ignore them. It's the round, smooth circle of light from the hole that you want to observe and measure.

Can Sound Travel through a Barrier?

TALK IT OVER:

Sound is vibration. The sounds that reach your ears travel as vibrations of the air. Can you hear sound through a barrier? Does a barrier affect how far away you can hear a sound?

GET: _____

- Outdoor space to work in
- Ball of white string
- Tent stake for soft ground (or tape for a paved surface)
- 1 or more willing listeners
- Blindfold

- Jingle bell
- Colored markers: black, red, and blue
- Large piece of cardboard
- Sharp scissors or knife
- Flexible, metal measuring tape (the kind carpenters use)

 GO

1. Find a large area outdoors where you can work. A grassy area in a park or a ball field is good, or you can use a paved playground.

2. Tie the string to the tent stake and put it into the ground at one end of your workspace. (If working on pavement, tape the string to the surface).

3. Ask a willing listener to stand at the tent stake (or tape) and wear a blindfold.

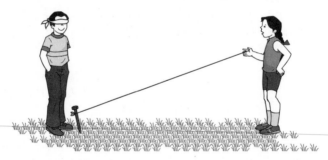

4. Tie the jingle bell to your finger. Ring the bell so the listener recognizes its sound.

5. Instruct the listener to raise a hand whenever he or she hears the jingle bell.

6. Start backing away from the listener, holding the loose end of the string in one hand and ringing the bell with the other. Every 1 or 2 meters (1 or 2 yards), ring the bell. Keep backing away, letting out more string and ringing until the listener no longer raises a hand.

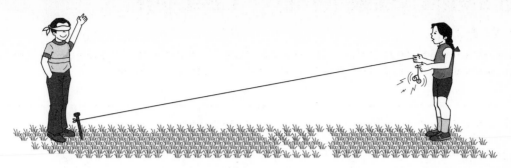

7. Flatten the string along the ground and make a black mark on it at that point. The black spot marks the limit at which the listener can hear the jingle bell.

8. Now return to the listener and repeat steps 5–6, holding the piece of cardboard in front of the bell, between you and the listener. When the listener no longer raises a hand, flatten the string along the ground and make a blue mark. The blue spot marks the distance at which the listener can hear the sound through the cardboard.

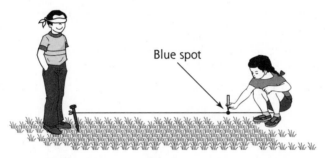

Blue spot

9. Ask an adult to use the scissors or a knife to cut a hole about the size of a quarter in the center of the cardboard. Repeat the experiment, holding the bell just behind the hole. Put a red mark on the string to indicate the distance at which the listener can hear the sound through the hole.

10. Using the metal measuring tape, measure the distances along the string to the black, blue, and red marks. Enter them in your data table under "Listener 1." Repeat the experiment with as many listeners as you can find to help you with your project. Use new string each time.

11. Calculate an average of all listeners for all three distances.

STAY SAFE:

Don't perform this experiment in a parking lot or in the street. Don't try to cut the hole in the cardboard yourself. Get an adult to help.

GO EASY

Use the "Go" procedure with two or three listeners, but don't calculate an average. Get an adult to help with the marking and measuring.

SOUND

GO FAR

Sound waves vary in their *frequency* and *amplitude*. Frequency determines pitch. Amplitude determines loudness.

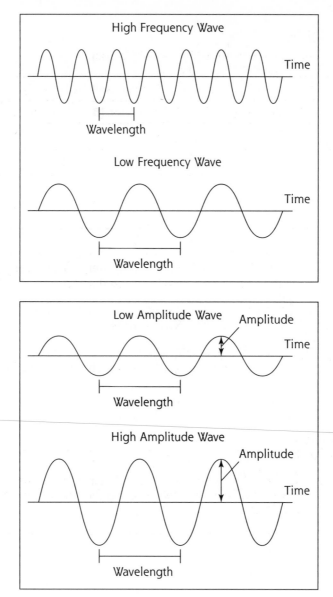

The jingle bell is a high frequency, low amplitude sound. Try the experiment with sounds of different frequencies and amplitudes. Also try substituting other barrier materials to see how they interact with different frequencies and amplitudes. You might also experiment with holes of different sizes and shapes. Or try several holes arranged in different patterns to see whether they impede or improve the average hearing distance.

SHOW YOUR RESULTS:

Put measurements in a data table like this for "Go" and "Go Easy":

Listener	Farthest Distance Bell Heard (cm)		
	No Barrier (Black)	Solid Barrier (Blue)	Hole in Barrier (Red)
1			
2			
3 . . . and so on			
Average (for "Go")			

For "Go Easy," make a bar graph showing the distances (on the vertical axis) for each of your listeners (on the horizontal axis). Use a color code to identify each listener. Write a few sentences to explain how the barrier (without and with the hole) affected listening distance.

For "Go," average the performance of all your listeners at each distance. Make a bar graph of averages. Write an explanation for the distance and barrier effects.

For "Go Far," make separate data tables for sounds of different frequencies and amplitudes. Make bar graphs to compare different kinds of barriers or different sizes, shapes, or configurations of holes.

Tips and Tricks

The jingle bell is recommended because it makes a soft sound that cannot be heard across too great a distance. If singing birds or distant traffic noises make hearing the bell difficult, try shaking a metal tack inside an aluminum soft drink can.

How Well Do People Judge the Direction of Sound?

TALK IT OVER:

Can you close your eyes and tell where a sound is coming from? How good a judge are you? How can you measure how well people judge the direction of sound?

GET:

- Large outdoor area to work in
- Balls of string in three colors: white, black, and red
- 2 tent stakes (for soft ground) or tape (for a paved surface)
- Flour
- Plastic bag
- Scissors
- Flexible, metal measuring tape (the kind carpenters use)
- 1 listener plus 2 other helpers
- Blindfold
- Protractor
- Jingle bell

1. Find a large area outdoors where you can work. A grassy area in a park or ball field is good. Or you can use a paved playground.

2. Tie all three colors of string to 1 tent stake and put it into the ground at the center of your workspace. (If working on pavement, tape the string to the surface).

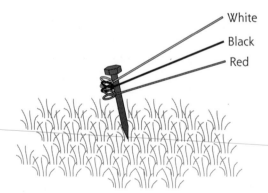

White
Black
Red

3. Put some flour in the plastic bag. Cut a small hole in a corner of the bag. Hold it shut for now so no flour leaks out.

4. You will now mark a circle with a radius of about 5 meters (5 yards). Here's how:

   a. Use the measuring tape to measure 5 meters (5 yards) of the white string.

   b. Walk away from the tent state (or taped string) until the string is taut.

   c. Release the hole in the bag of flour and walk slowly around the stake, keeping the string taut and allowing the flour to fall to the ground.

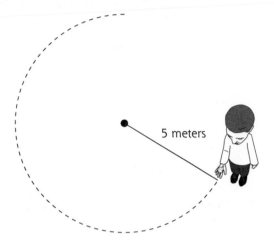

5. Tie the white string to another tent stake and push it into the ground at a fixed point on the circle (or tape it down). The white string will not move again.

6. Ask the listener to stand in the center of the circle and wear the blindfold. Position the listener facing the white line. Have the listener hold the protractor.

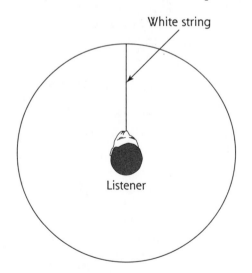

SOUND

7. Tie a jingle bell to your finger. Ring the bell so the listener knows what to listen for.

8. Instruct the listener to point toward the sound of the jingle bell whenever he or she hears it.

9. When the experiment begins, you and at least two other people start moving randomly (and silently!) around the circle. (You want to confuse the listener about the source and direction of the sound.) After a few seconds, signal everyone to stop. Then ring the jingle bell. The listener points a finger toward the exact spot where the sound seems to be coming from.

10. Now, you and the listener must not move while one of your helpers pulls the black string from the center of the circle to you. The other helper pulls the red string to the outer circle along the exact line in which the listener is pointing, like this:

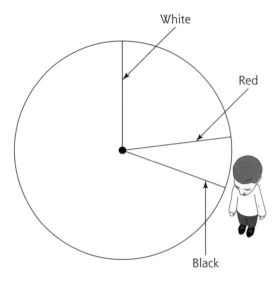

11. Now the listener removes the blindfold and measures two angles using the protractor. The first is the angle from which the sound actually came, measured from the white, stationary baseline to the black string. The second is the angle that the listener perceived, from the white baseline to the red string. Measure the angles in a *clockwise* direction from the white string.

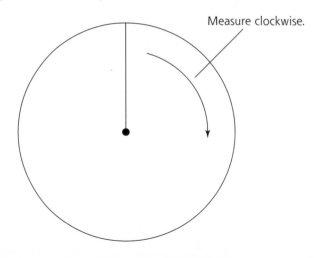

Here are some examples:

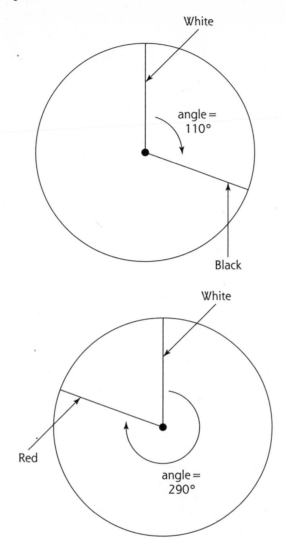

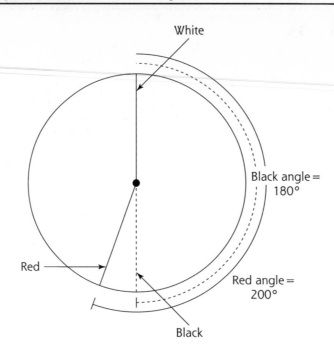

White

Black angle =
180°

Red

Red angle =
200°

Black

12. Continue with the same listener, trying many more angles and getting many more measurements. For each measurement, subtract to find the *error*:

guessed angle – actual angle = error

13. Ignore the sign of the error. Look only at its *absolute value*. The smaller the error, the more accurately the listener judged the sound's direction.

14. Switch roles and let someone else be the listener. Gather as much data as you can with as many different angles and listeners as possible.

GO EASY

Work with only one listener and get an adult to help measure the angles and calculate the error. Test four angles as sound sources: 0°, 90°, 180°, and 270° (from the white string to the bell, clockwise, in relation to the listener).

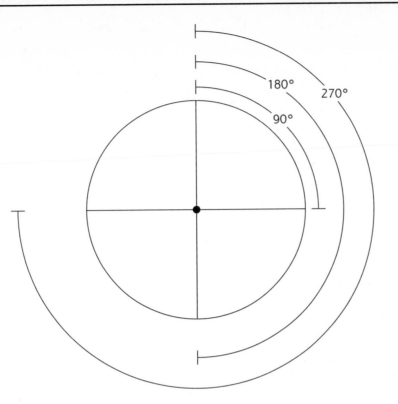

GO FAR

Human ears open to the sides and slightly forward. Use that fact to state and test a hypothesis about which angles will produce the best (or worst) results on the directional hearing test outlined in "Go."

SHOW YOUR RESULTS:

Put angles in a data table like this for "Go Easy":

Angle of Sound	Angle Listener Guessed	Difference (Error)
0°		
90°		
180°		
270°		

Make a bar graph showing the error at each angle tested. See whether the heights of the bars support any conclusions.

For "Go," and "Go Far," use the same data table, but add other angles. Make a data table for each listener you test. Then use a *scatterplot* to look for a possible *correlation* between the actual angle and the calculated error. (*Correlate* means vary together in some predictable way.) To make a scatterplot, put the actual angle along the horizontal axis. Put the calculated error on the vertical axis. Then, for each listener at each angle you tested, find the point where the actual angle and the error intersect. Put a dot at that point. For example, if your first angle was 90° and your listener missed it by 15°, your first dot would be placed like this:

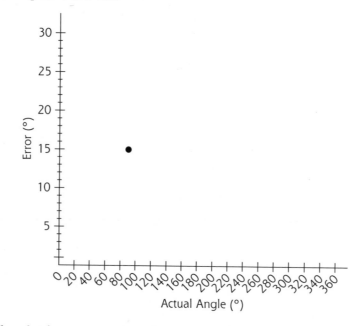

After you have made a dot for every angle and every error (across all listeners), look at where the dots lie. You may see a pattern that suggests that errors are greater or less at certain sound-source angles. If you see a pattern, try to explain it.

Tips and Tricks

Don't worry that the listener is measuring angles close to the center of the large circle. An angle is the same at any distance.

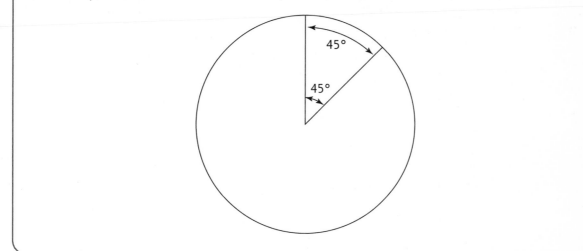

How Does the Length of a Vibrating Column Affect Pitch?

TALK IT OVER:

Sound travels in waves. Shorter wavelengths have a higher *frequency,* which your brain detects as a higher pitch.

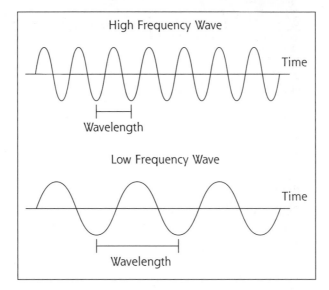

On a violin, shortening the length of a string raises the pitch of the sound. In an organ, the short pipes make higher pitched sounds than the long pipes. How can you investigate the effect of length on the frequency of sound waves?

GET: _____

- Long piece of bamboo*
- Saw
- Thread
- Tape
- Table

- Chopstick
- Access to a piano or keyboard instrument
- Sound frequency computer software (optional for "Go Far")*

GO

1. Ask an adult to use a saw to cut the bamboo into lengths for you. Vary the lengths in a pre-determined way. You might try increments of 5 cm (2 inches).

2. Tie threads around the middles of the bamboo pieces. Tape the threads to the edge of a table so the pieces hang freely, like this:

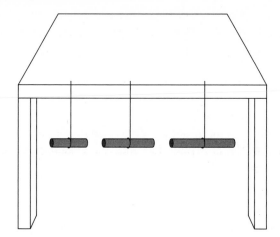

3. One at a time, strike the pieces with the chopstick. Listen closely to the pitch you hear. Try to match it to a pitch you play on a piano or keyboard instrument.

4. Find a standard table of the frequencies and wavelengths of musical notes. There are many of them on the Internet. They look like this one, which shows the notes around middle C on the piano:

Note on piano	Frequency (Hertz)	Wavelength (in meters)
G	196	1.7
G# / A♭	208	1.6
A	220	1.5
A# / B♭	233	1.5
B	247	1.4
Middle C	262	1.3
C# / D♭	277	1.2
D	294	1.2
D# / E♭	311	1.1
E	330	1.0
F	349	1.0
F# / G♭	370	0.9

5. For each of the lengths you test, decide which note on the piano or keyboard matches its pitch most closely. Look up that note in the table. Record the known frequency and wavelength.

STAY SAFE:

Don't do the sawing yourself. Get an adult to cut the bamboo pieces for you. Be careful with the cut ends. They can be sharp.

GO EASY

Use only three lengths of bamboo: long, medium, and short. Try to match the pitches you hear to the notes you find on a piano or keyboard. Try to state in a single sentence how the length of a vibrating column (which is what your pipe is) affects pitch.

GO FAR

Get and learn to use a computer software program* that uses a Fast Fourier Transform to analyze the frequencies of sound. Get computer frequency analyses from the bamboo pieces you test. See how the computer analysis compares with what you assessed using only your ears and a table of frequencies. Once you master the testing procedure and the software, try analyzing the sounds other materials make. You might try plastic or aluminum pipe or solid rods of steel or copper.

SHOW YOUR RESULTS:

For "Go" and "Go Easy," put the note you think you hear—your best guess of pitch—into a data table like this one. Add the frequencies and wavelengths you look up in a standard table.

Length of Piece	Note I Think It Makes	Frequency (from Table, in Hertz)	Wavelength (from Table, in Meters)
5 cm			
10 cm			
15 cm . . . and so on			

Make a bar or line graph with the length of the piece on the horizontal axis and either frequency or wavelength on the vertical axis. Write a few sentences telling how they relate.

For "Go Far," use similar data tables and graphs, but use the analyses from your computer program to determine frequency and wavelength. If you investigate other materials, write about how they differ in the wavelengths they produce.

Tips and Tricks

- Here's a quick and easy way to demonstrate the same principle. Put a straw in a glass of water. Pull back your lower lip and blow down into the straw, like this.

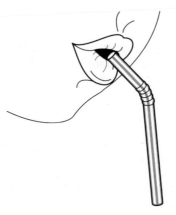

Once you can make a whistling sound, move the straw up and down in the water. It works just like a trombone.

- Your computer analysis will probably show that your sounds are a mix of frequencies. That explains, in part, why middle C on a piano and middle C on a violin are the same pitch but sound so different.

How Does the Loudness of Sound Vary in a Room?

TALK IT OVER:

Is it easier to hear the teacher in some classrooms than in others? What about hearing music in an auditorium or the announcer in a gymnasium? Sound engineers measure the intensity of sound in a unit called the *decibel*. In general, the higher the decibel level of a sound, the louder it seems. You can use a sound-level meter to measure the decibel level of a sound from a single source. That way, you can map a room to see how well sound can be heard at different places in it.

GET:

- Permission to take sound-level readings in one or more rooms (perhaps classrooms) when they are not in use
- Portable CD player and CD
- Floor plan or blueprint of rooms (optional)

- Drawing materials
- Sound-level meter*
- Flexible, metal measuring tape (the kind carpenters use)

GO

1. Select a room to study. You might study a room in your home or a classroom at school. Ask permission to work in the room.

2. Choose a CD to use as your sound source. You may want to play music. Alternatively, if you are interested in how easily a person's voice is heard in a room, you might want to use an audio book.

3. Study the floor plan of the room in advance, if you can get one. Measure the length, width, and ceiling height of the room. Draw a sketch of the room's design. Make drawings or notes of any important features, such as acoustical ceiling tiles, stone walls, or tiled or carpeted floors. Also make note of furniture such as desks or chairs that may affect sound distribution in the room.

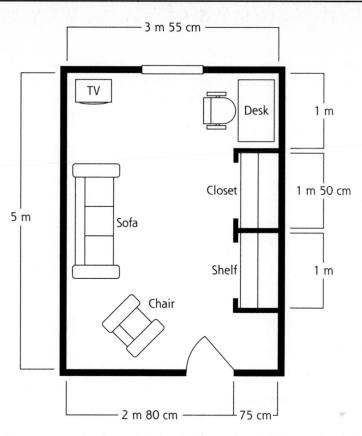

4. Set the CD in a spot in the room. Start it playing. Use your sound-level meter to take a reading, in decibels, of the intensity of the sound at its source.

5. Without altering the volume of the sound source, take readings at other points in the room. Measure the distance from the source using your flexible, metal measuring tape. Make a map of your points and readings.

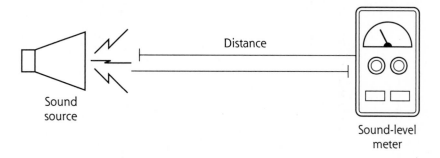

6. Depending on your project plan, you can investigate other rooms or other sound sources. Try to relate any similarities and differences to the design, layout, or construction of the rooms.

SOUND

STAY SAFE:

Loud noises destroy tiny hair cells in the inner ear that send sound messages through the auditory nerve to the brain. Once those cells die, they never grow back. It takes only ½ hour at a rock concert or listening to a stereo headset set at full blast (about 110 decibels) to impair your hearing permanently.

GO EASY

Ask an adult to help you learn to use the sound-level meter. You'll need help with measuring the room and recording readings, too.

GO FAR

In real life, you often hear sounds not from a single source, but from two or more at the same time. What does this mean in terms of decibel readings? Use your sound-level meter and a modification of the "Go" procedure to answer the following question: Does the intensity of two sounds equal their sum in decibels?

SHOW YOUR RESULTS:

For each room you investigate, you should end up with a map that looks something like this:

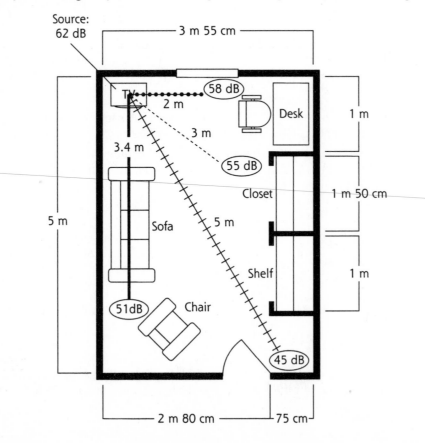

Make a line graph that relates distance from the source (on the horizontal axis) to the decibel levels you recorded with your sound-level meter (on the vertical axis).

For "Go Far," make maps and graphs that compare the sound-level readings you record with one, two, or more sound sources. Do some research and find the mathematical formula that predicts the loudness of sounds from additive sources. Do your findings match the formula?

For all projects, display your room maps along with floor plans if you have them. Try to relate your readings to the room's construction or to the design and layout of its contents.

Tips and Tricks

- Background sounds or sounds entering the room from outside sources can affect your readings. Try to work in the room when it is as quiet as possible.
- Songs on a music CD or actors' voices on an audio book can vary in loudness. Select a sound source that maintains a consistent intensity throughout.

SOUND

Does Distance Affect a Sound-Activated Finder?

TALK IT OVER:

A sound-activated *finder* is a popular and inexpensive gadget for locating misplaced objects. Clap your hands and a sound sensor on the finder starts a light flashing or a beeper beeping. This is a handy way to find lost keys, remote controls, cellphones—just about anything that can be attached to the finder. But will such finders work from long distances? in rooms full of furniture? when lost items are buried under piles of clothes or school books? How can you find out?

GET:

- Large, flat working space indoors or outdoors
- Tape recorder or way to record a sound on a CD
- Tape or CD player
- Sound-activated "finder"*
- Flexible metal measuring tape (the kind carpenters use)
- Drawing materials

GO

1. Find a place where you can experiment on your finder without objects or barriers getting in the way. An open, grassy spot in a park works well. Indoors, a gymnasium is your best choice. If necessary, ask permission to use the site.

2. Tape-record or make a CD of your clapping in whatever pattern is required by your sound-activated finder. You are doing this so you will use exactly the same pitch, pattern, and volume every time your test your finder.

3. In your work area, place your finder at a convenient spot. Move about 3 meters (3 yards) away in any direction, using your flexible tape to measure the distance.

4. Make a sketch to show where you are in relation to the finder. Play the sound of hands clapping. Record how the finder responds.

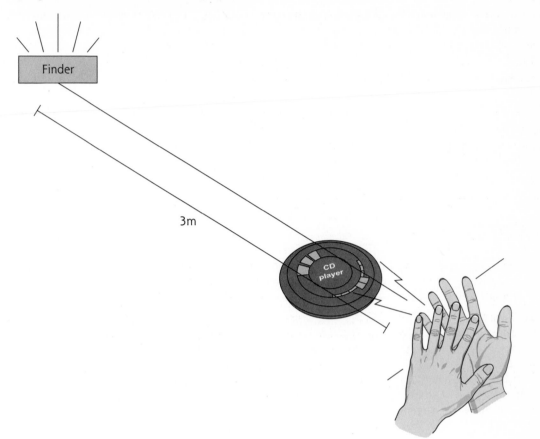

5. Without moving the finder, turn it off. Don't change the volume of the taped sound. Move to another location and repeat step 4.

6. Keep doing this until you have tested a large number of angles and distances in your study area.

7. If you wish, repeat the test with a pillow or book over the finder or a barrier, such as a sheet of cardboard, held between you and the finder.

STAY SAFE:

About the only way to get hurt in this experiment is to trip over the measuring tape or get sunburned working outdoors. You know how to prevent both.

GO EASY

Use the "Go" procedure through step 6. Ask an adult to help you with the measuring and sketching.

GO FAR

Build your own sound-activated switch from a kit*. You'll need a soldering iron and someone to show you how to use it. That's all the help you'll need to build a sound-activated switch. Choose a model that allows you to adjust its sensitivity so it responds to the softest sound or only to a very loud sound. You might even be able to engineer the switch to respond to a sound other than clapping.

SHOW YOUR RESULTS:

Summarize your observations in a data table like this for "Go Easy" and "Go":

Distance (in meters)	Finder Response
3	
6	
9 (or distances of your choice)	

Display your sketches. State a conclusion about your finder's distance limits, if you found any. You may also report the results of other experiments using pillows, barriers, or any other variable you chose to test.

For "Go Far," show the switch you built and explain its operation in your project report. Try to use experimental data to answer the following question: How does adjusting the sensitivity on the sound-activated switch affect response distance?

Tips and Tricks

- Keep fresh batteries in your finder throughout the testing. Low batteries could affect its operation.
- The "Go" procedure asks you to measure only the horizontal distance from the finder. But you'll have a better project if you also measure and report any vertical difference between the sound source and the finder, for example:

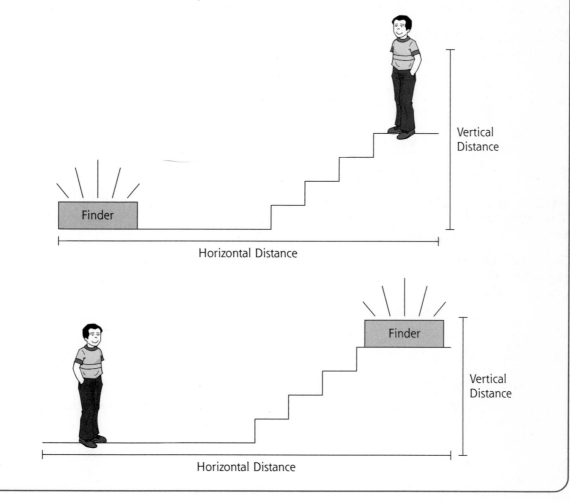

SOUND

Do Temperature and Humidity Affect How Long Static Charges Last?

TALK IT OVER:

Have you ever noticed that socks cling to your clothes and to each other when they come out of the dryer? If so, you have noticed *static electricity*. It is an electrical charge that builds up in an object when electrons move to or from its surface. In the case of socks in the dryer, opposite charges (+ and –) build up and attract, causing the pieces to cling.

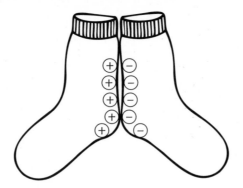

You can see the effects of static electricity and measure how long a static charge lasts.

GET:

- Thermometer with a humidity dial
- 2 round balloons
- String
- Ruler
- Table

- Tape
- Rubber ball
- Silk or polyester scarf or fabric piece
- Rubber band
- Stopwatch

GO

1. Note and record the time, date, temperature, and humidity.
2. Blow up 2 round balloons to approximately the same size. Tie them off. Attach a piece of string about 30 cm (12 in.) long to each balloon.

3. Tape the strings to the tabletop, so the balloons hang over the edge. One should be in line with the table leg. Make them hang about 10 cm (4 in.) apart.

4. Tape the balloon near the table leg to it. Tape it securely, so it cannot move.

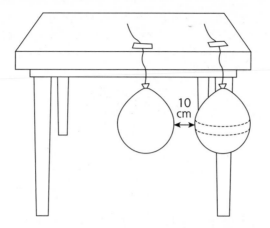

5. Put the rubber ball inside the scarf and secure it with the rubber band, like this:

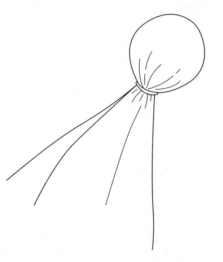

6. Run the covered ball over the moveable balloon exactly 20 times. For each rub, move the ball from the top to the bottom of the balloon. Turn the balloon as you go so you are sure you rub the entire surface of the balloon.

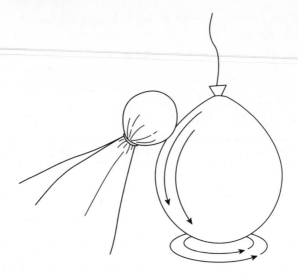

7. Let go and notice what happens. When the moveable balloon sticks to the stationary balloon, start the stopwatch.

8. Stop the stopwatch when the moveable balloon falls away. (Be patient. This could take a while.)

9. Repeat this experiment at other days and times, when the temperature and humidity vary.

STAY SAFE:

Rub a balloon on your hair and you may hear a crackle or feel your hair stand on end. The static charge won't hurt you, but the sound will give you a good idea of what static electricity is all about.

GO EASY

Instead of investigating temperature and humidity, you can compare different materials used to rub the balloon to answer the following question: Does one material produce a longer lasting static charge than another? Try comparing wool, silk, polyester, plastic wrap, and any other rubbing materials you can think of.

GO FAR

Conduct the experiment indoors and outdoors under as wide a range of temperatures and humidities as possible.

SHOW YOUR RESULTS:

Put times in a data table like this for "Go Easy":

Material Tested	How Long the Charge Lasted (in Minutes)
Wool	
Silk	
Polyester	

Make a bar graph that compares the materials you tried (on the horizontal axis) by how long the charges they induced lasted (on the vertical axis).

For "Go," use a data table like this. Complete a column for every trial of the experiment.

How Long the Charged Lasted (in Minutes)				
Date____ Time____ Temperature____ Humidity____	Date____ Time____ Temperature____ Humidity____	Date____ Time____ Temperature____ Humidity____	Date____ Time____ Temperature____ Humidity____	Date____ Time____ Temperature____ Humidity____

Make a line graph showing how long the charge lasted (on the vertical axis) by the temperature (on the horizontal). Make a separate graph of the same type for humidity. See whether the slopes of the lines reveal anything about the effects of either temperature or humidity on how long a static charge lasts.

For "Go Far," make a scatterplot of your data to look for possible *correlations* between temperature, humidity, and how long a static charge lasts. (*Correlate* means vary together in some predictable way.) If, for example, static charges last longer on warm days, then the correlation between those two variables would be positive. If they last longer on cold days, then the correlation would be negative. If the numbers are random in relation to each other, then there is no correlation.

ELECTRICITY

The first step toward finding a correlation is a *scatterplot* graph. Use your data to make the graph. Put temperature or humidity along the horizontal axis. Put the time the charge lasted on the vertical. Then, for each trial, find the point where temperature (or humidity) and charge-time intersect. Put a dot at that point. For example, if the humidity was 40 percent and your charge lasted 50 minutes, your first dot would be placed like this:

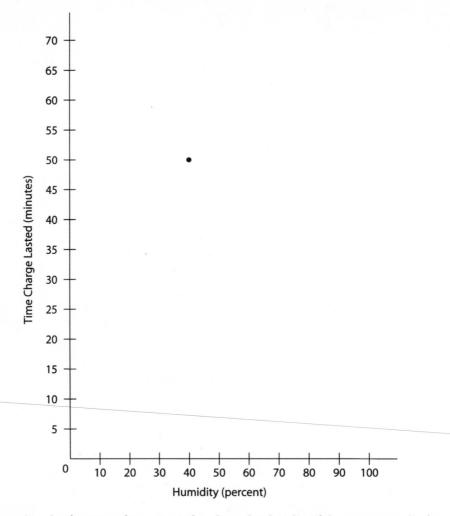

After you have made a dot for every data set, study where the dots lie. If they appear to lie (more or less) along a straight line, then draw it. If your line slants upward, you *may* have a positive correlation. If it slants down, you *may* have a negative correlation. If the points are so spread out that no line seems to match them, you *may* have found that temperature (or humidity) and charge-time are not correlated.

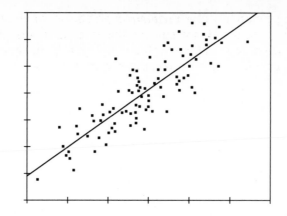

Possible Positive Correlation

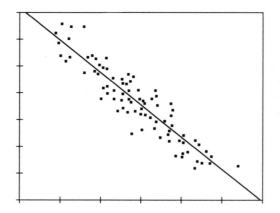

Possible Negative Correlation

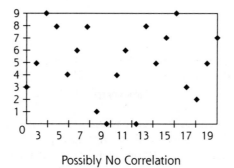

Possibly No Correlation

Tips and Tricks

- If you can't find scarves or fabric pieces to rub on your balloons, try jackets, shirts, socks, or hats. Check the label to determine fiber content.
- If you don't have a thermometer with a humidity dial, check your local weather report online at http://weather.noaa.gov.
- Don't touch your balloons while you are timing. You'll take away some of the charge. Even walking by or fanning the balloons with air can make a difference, so set up your experiment out of drafts and high-traffic areas.

Does Electricity Move Better through Thick Wires or Thin Ones?

TALK IT OVER:

Why do you plug lamps, washing machines, and other electrical appliances into wall sockets? Inside the cords of such devices are metal wires that electric current moves through. Can current move faster, better, or easier if the wires are thick or thin?

GET:

- Plastic straw
- 2 D batteries
- Scissors
- Electrical tape
- A medium steel wool pad
- 2 flashlight bulbs

GO

1. Cut 2 pieces of straw the same length as the batteries. Tape them to the batteries, like this:

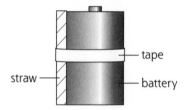

2. Pull a few strands from the steel wool pad. Roll them lengthwise between your hands (as you would modeling clay) to make a thin roll of wire. Repeat, but with more strands, to make a thicker wire. Thread the wires through the straws, leaving exposed ends, like this:

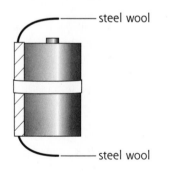

3. Tape one end of each wire to the flat end (negative terminal) of a battery, like this:

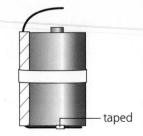

4. Twist the other end of each steel wire around a bulb and secure with tape. Don't let the tape cover the base of the bulb.

5. Stand the 2 batteries side by side. Holding the bulbs by the glass part, touch the base of the bulb to the "bump" on the positive terminal of the battery, like this:

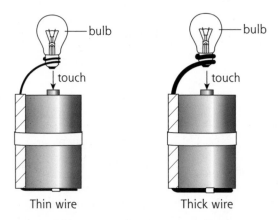

Thin wire   Thick wire

6. Which bulb glows brighter? Suggest a reason to explain what you see.

7. As soon as you see a difference, pull the bulbs away from the battery terminals. Hold them too long and you'll burn out the bulb and run down the battery.

STAY SAFE:

Hold the bulbs only by the glass part. Don't touch the base of the bulb or the steel wool. They get hot!

GO EASY

What materials allow electric current to move? What materials slow or stop it? Use the same setup as above, but with only one battery and bulb. Don't use steel wool. Instead, thread the materials you want to test through the straw and observe whether the bulb lights. You might try string, plastic wrap, copper wire, or a strip of aluminum foil.

GO FAR

The opposition of a material to the flow of an electrical current is called *resistance*. It is measured in ohms. The greater the resistance (the larger the number of ohms), the less current flows. To learn more about resistance and demonstrate its effects, you can use the "Go" procedure to

- Test electrical wires of different thicknesses (called *gauge*) for their resistance
- Compare the resistances of wires made of different metals
- Experiment to find out how temperature affects resistance

You might also purchase an inexpensive electrical tester* and use it to measure resistance in electrical circuits you build.

SHOW YOUR RESULTS:

Put check marks in a data table like this for "Go Easy":

Material Tested	It Lights	It Doesn't Light

For "Go," draw diagrams of your setups and observations. Write a few sentences telling what you saw and giving your explanation. Put your setups with your display so others can try the experiment for themselves.

For "Go Far," make a bar graph showing how the variable you studied relates to resistance. For example, you might make a bar graph of the ohms of resistance you measured using different gauges of copper wire.*

Tips and
Tricks

Depleted batteries and burned out bulbs can prevent bulbs from lighting, but if you're working with new materials and getting no glow, something is probably loose somewhere. Check taped connections to make sure wires are firmly attached to battery and bulb.

ELECTRICITY

Which Brand of Batteries Is Stronger or Lasts Longer?

TALK IT OVER:

Some brands of batteries advertise that they are stronger or last longer than other brands. How can you test their claim?

GET:

- 2 identical flashlights with new bulbs
- 2 different brands of batteries, new, of the right size for the flashlights
- Large, felt-tip marker
- Electrical tester*
- Watch or clock
- Sunprint Kit (optional for "Go Far")*

GO

1. Start this experiment in the morning, so you can work on it all day if you need to. Make sure all your batteries are new and fresh. Check the expiration dates printed on the packages.

2. Using the marker, put a letter on the side of each battery. Letter them A, B, C, D, and so on.

3. Following the manufacturer's directions for the electrical tester, check the output of each battery. Record the numbers in a table.

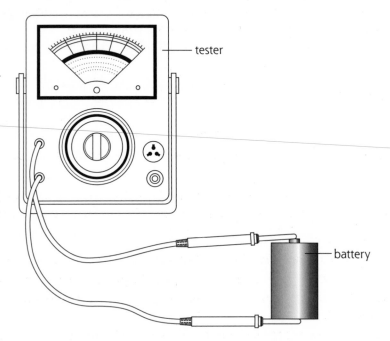

tester

battery

4. Load the batteries in the flashlights, using a different brand for each flashlight. Note the letters on the batteries you put in each flashlight and the order you put them in (because most flashlights require more than one battery).

5. Switch on the flashlights and note the time. Allow them to burn for 30 minutes.

6. Turn off the flashlights. Remove the batteries and test each with the electrical tester. Record the time and the reading.

7. Return the batteries to their same flashlights and same positions. Let them burn for another 30 minutes. Then turn off, remove, remeasure, and reload. Keep doing this every 30 minutes for several hours.

STAY SAFE:

The batteries can't hurt you. The amount of electricity they discharge is too small. Flashlights' bulbs can, however, get hot. Pick up flashlights only by their handles.

GO EASY

The "Go" procedure will work for you.

GO FAR

Use the "Go" procedure to test several different brands. Test each brand three times and average your results.

You can improve your project with pictures that show differences in the intensity of the lights at different times. If, for example, you notice that 1 light is looking dimmer than another at 11:30 a.m., do this:

1. Turn off the flashlights.

2. On a table close to a wall, place the flashlights at least 60 cm (2 feet) apart.

3. In front of each flashlight, tape to the wall a piece of light-sensitive paper from a Sunprint Kit*.

4. Move the flashlights close to the paper. Their light should be no more than 1 cm (less than ½ inch) from the wall.

5. Turn the flashlights on. Let them shine on the paper for 30 minutes or more. (You may need to try this several times, using more or less time. The time depends on how bright the lights are.)

6. Process the photosensitive paper in water as the package directs.

7. The brighter the light, the *darker* the circle that appears on the paper.

8. To get numbers that will allow you to compare the lights, make a black-and-white photocopy of your papers. (Set the copy machine to make a light copy.) Then find the numbers on your grayscale (See "How to Make a Grayscale" in Part III) that most closely match the dark spots your flashlights made on the paper. The higher the number, the brighter the light was.

SHOW YOUR RESULTS:

Put your electrical tester readings in a data table like this for "Go" and "Go Easy":

Battery Brand: Letter	Electrical Tester Reading (in volts)				
	9:00 a.m.	9:30 a.m.	10:00 a.m.	10.30 a.m.	11:00 a.m. . . . and so on
HappyBat: A					
HappyBat: B . . . and so on					
SadBat: E					
SadBat: F . . . and so on					

For "Go Far," make tables that compare several brands. Add columns to show multiple trials and your calculated averages.

Make line graphs from the tables. Show how the electrical tester readings changed over the time of the experiment. Put volts on the vertical axis. Put time on the horizontal axis. Use different colors of lines for different brands of batteries.

State a brief conclusion that compares brands of batteries and how long they last. If you can, use number relationships in your conclusion. For example, you might find that HappyBat's readings were 20 percent higher than SadBat's readings throughout your experiment.

Tips and Tricks

- At the beginning of the experiment, all the batteries of the same brand should have nearly the same reading on the tester—although different brands may not. If your batteries vary too much, buy fresh ones.

- The 30-minute measurement interval in "Go" works best for flashlights that use 2 or 4 large, size D batteries. Smaller flashlights that use AA batteries may run down faster. Measure every 10–15 minutes.

- If a flashlight bulb burns out before the battery goes dead, stop the experiment. Get new bulbs in all the flashlights and start over.

Does the Sun's Angle Affect the Output of a Solar Cell?

TALK IT OVER:

A solar cell changes energy from the sun into electrical energy. Does the angle of the sun striking the solar cell affect how much electricity the cell puts out? How can you find out?

GET: _____

- Piece of cardboard, about 8½ in. x 11 in.
- Glue
- Solar cell*
- Electrical tape
- Electrical tester* (with a 0-250mA DC range)

- Sunny day
- Books
- Protractor
- Modeling clay
- Drawing materials

GO

1. Glue the solar cell to the cardboard, black side down.

2. Attach the red wire from the solar cell to the red lead from the electrical tester. Secure with electrical tape.

3. Tape the black wire from the solar cell to the cardboard, with its bare end exposed. Make sure you can touch the bare wire with the tip of the black lead from the electrical tester.

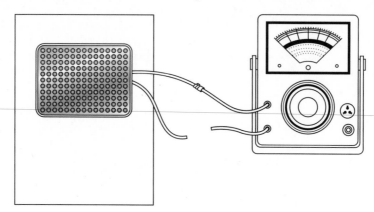

4. Outside on a sunny day, turn the solar cell toward the sun. Put a book under an end of the cardboard. Using the protractor, find a propping position that will put your solar cell at a 10° angle to the table or ground. If necessary, stabilize the cardboard with a lump of modeling clay.

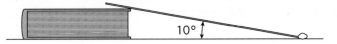

5. Turn on the electrical tester and set it to read in the 0–250mA DC range. Touch the black lead from the tester to the black wire from the solar cell. Read and record the number on the electrical tester.

6. Reposition the solar cell at 20° and test again. Repeat for 30°, 40°, and so on until your cell is perpendicular to the ground at 90°.

STAY SAFE:

Never look at the sun. It can blind you. Wear sunscreen, hat, and protective clothing whenever you are in the sun. The sun's radiation causes wrinkling, spotting, and skin cancer.

GO EASY

Get an adult's help with setting up the cell, using the protractor, and reading the tester. Test your solar cell at 30°, 60°, and 90° only.

GO FAR

The *angle of incidence* is only one of many factors that affect the output of a solar, or *photovoltaic,* cell. (It is not the angle of the cell in relation to the ground that we used in this experiment, but the angle of the sun's rays falling on the solar cell.)

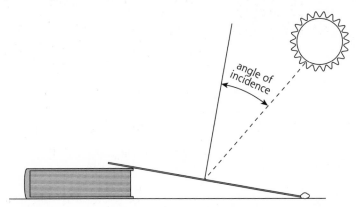

Design and carry out experiments to determine how other variables, such as air temperature, clouds, shade, reflective surfaces, and compass direction, change the output of your solar cell.

ELECTRICITY

SHOW YOUR RESULTS:

Put your electrical tester readings in a data table like this for "Go Easy":

Angle	Output (in mA)
30°	
60°	
90°	

For "Go," add rows for the other angles you tried. For both "Go Easy" and "Go," make a bar or line graph that shows how the solar cell's output (on the vertical axis) changes with the angle (on the horizontal axis). Write a few sentences summarizing any differences you observed and explaining the reasons for them.

For "Go Far," make data tables and graphs for the variables you measure. State conclusions about how each factor you studied affects solar cell output.

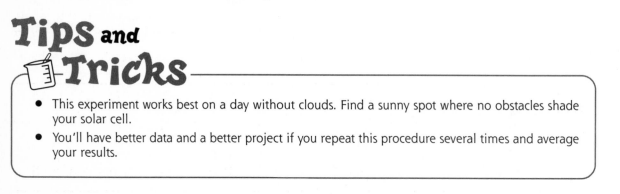

Tips and Tricks

- This experiment works best on a day without clouds. Find a sunny spot where no obstacles shade your solar cell.
- You'll have better data and a better project if you repeat this procedure several times and average your results.

Does a Fresnel Lens Affect the Output of a Solar Cell?

TALK IT OVER:

In a solar cell, the energy in sunlight is converted directly into electricity. How might a solar cell be designed to make the most electricity possible? A *Fresnel lens* (pronounced freh-NEL—the "s" is silent) is a thin, flat lens made by cutting concentric circular grooves into a glass or plastic surface.

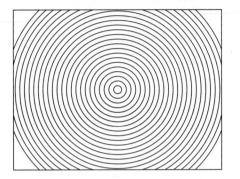

The grooves act like prisms; they bend and focus light. What effect might a Fresnel lens have on the output of a solar cell? How can you find out?

GET:

- Picture frame, with glass plate and removable cardboard back with hinged support
- Solar cell*
- Tape or glue
- Electrical tester (with a 0–250mA DC range) *
- Electrical tape
- Sunny spot to work in
- Modeling clay
- Ruler (metric)
- Fresnel lens (also called a magnifying sheet)*

GO

1. Remove the glass from the picture frame. Also remove the cardboard backing with its hinged support. Glue or tape the solar cell to the cardboard, like this:

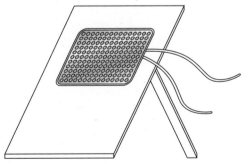

2. With electrical tape, connect the red and black output wires from the solar cell to the red and black probes of the electrical tester. Do not turn the tester on.

3. Set the solar cell in the sun. Bend the cardboard and support so you get a good angle of sunlight on the solar cell. (See the preceding project: "Does the sun's angle affect the output of a solar cell?") Hold in place with a lump of clay.

4. Turn on the tester. Set it to the 0–250mA DC range. Read the output of the cell. Hold the plain glass plate (from the picture frame) 1 cm (½ inch) in front of the solar cell. Read the output on the tester.

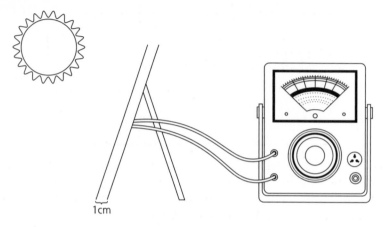

5. Move to 2 cm and read again. Continue moving 1 cm (½ inch) at a time and taking readings until the glass plate is 15 cm (6 inches) from the cell.

6. Without changing the position of the solar cell, repeat steps 4 and 5 using the Fresnel lens (magnifying sheet) instead of the glass. Turn its smooth side to face the sun.

STAY SAFE:

Wear sunscreen, hat, and protective clothing when you are in the sun. The sun's radiation causes wrinkling, spotting, and skin cancer. Never look at the sun. It can blind you. Be careful of the edges on the glass, because they can be sharp.

GO EASY

The "Go" procedure will work for you. Take output readings at 1, 5, 10, and 15 cm (½, 2, 4, and 6 inches) only. Get an adult's help with the setup, measuring, and recording.

GO FAR

Efficiency is a mathematical measure of how well the solar panel changes the sun's light to electricity. A panel with 10 percent efficiency, for example, changes 10 percent of the light energy that hits it into useable electrical energy. Do some research on the Internet or in your library to find out how to estimate the amount of light energy that hits your solar panel. Then calculate percent efficiency using the "Go" procedure. Modify your setup to obtain the maximum efficiency.

SHOW YOUR RESULTS:

Put data in a table like this for "Go Easy":

	Distance (in cm)	Output (mA)
Plain glass	1	
	5	
	10	
	15	
Fresnel lens	1	
	5	
	10	
	15	

For "Go," add rows for the intermediate distances at 1-cm intervals. For "Go" and "Go Easy," make bar graphs that compare the output of the solar cell using plain glass and the Fresnel lens. For "Go," make a line graph of outputs (on the vertical axis) by distance (on the horizontal axis). Use different colors of lines to compare plain glass and the Fresnel lens.

For "Go Far," calculate efficiencies using different angles and arrangements of the cell and the Fresnel lens. Make bar and line graphs to show under which conditions maximal efficiency was achieved.

Tips and Tricks

- Be careful with your Fresnel lens. It can focus a spot of light energy hot enough to start a fire!
- Extend your project by turning your Fresnel lens over. Does it matter which side faces the sun?

ELECTRICITY

How Does a Compass Work?

TALK IT OVER:

What is a compass? What is it used for? How and why does it work? You can make your own compass to answer these questions.

GET: _____

- Modeling clay
- Drinking glass
- 2 bamboo skewers
- Rubber band
- 3 small bar magnets* or 1 long bar magnet
- Red nail polish

- Thread, about 15-cm piece
- Graph paper
- Tape
- Black, red, and green markers
- Ruler
- Map or compass (optional)

 GO

1. Put a lump of modeling clay in a drinking glass. Stick a bamboo skewer upright in it.

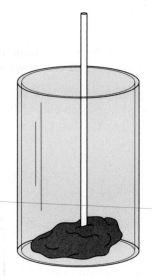

2. Put another skewer across the top of the glass. Loop the rubber band around both skewers several times so they stay together, but the one resting on the drinking glass edge can still turn freely.

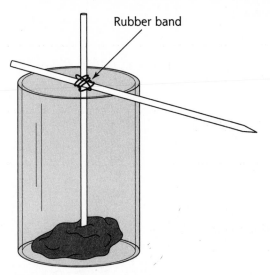

Rubber band

3. Put the 3 bar magnets together so they make one long magnet (or use one long bar magnet). Put a dot of red nail polish at one end so you know which end is which.

4. Tie one end of the thread around the middle of the magnet. Tie the other end to the skewer. The magnet should hang level and balanced, while still able to swing freely, like this:

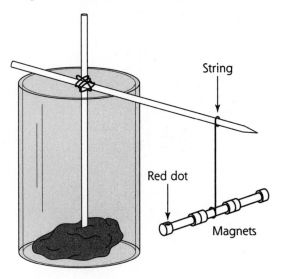

String

Red dot

Magnets

5. Tape a sheet of graph paper to the table.

6. Set the glass on the paper, with its base centered at the left edge of the paper, like this:

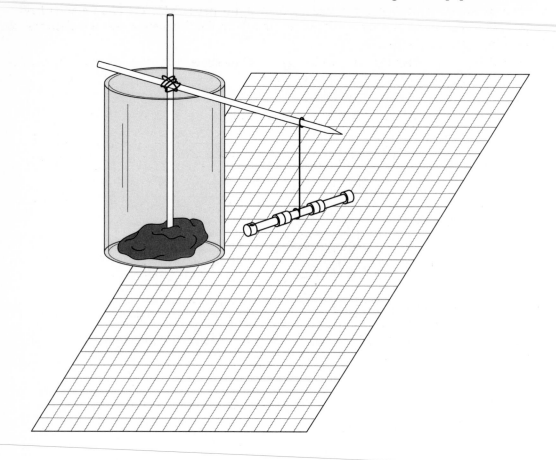

7. With the black marker, draw around the base of the glass. Keep the glass in this circle throughout the experiment.

8. Turn the skewer so it points in any direction over the paper. With the black marker held straight down beside the skewer, make two marks on the paper: one near the glass and one near the tip of the skewer.

9. With the ruler, connect the two black dots. This line shows where you pointed the skewer.

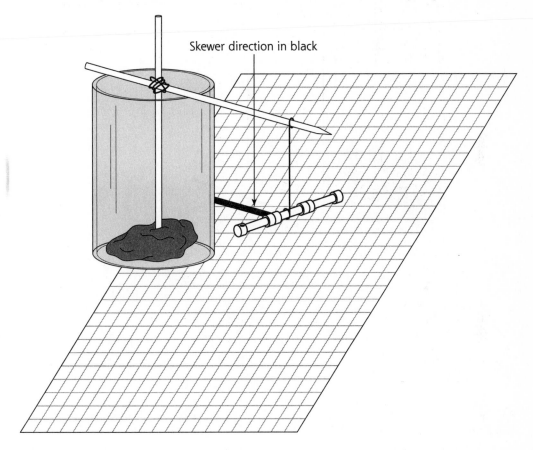

Skewer direction in black

10. Let the magnet swing freely. When it stops, make a red mark on the graph paper under the red-dotted end of the magnet. Make a green mark directly beneath the other end. Use the ruler and the red marker to connect the points with a straight line. Make an arrow point on the red dot end of the line, like this:

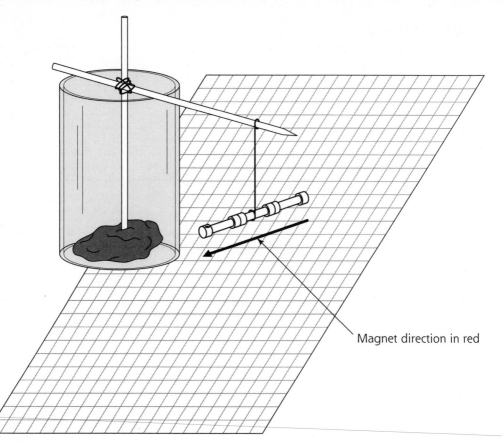

Magnet direction in red

11. Repeat steps 8–10 several times more, pointing the skewer in a different direction each time. You should end up with a black line and a red arrow for every trial of the experiment.

12. Try to figure out where your red arrows are pointing. Use a map or compass for help if you need to.

STAY SAFE:

Nothing here is dangerous, but a magnet can harm your compass. Don't keep them close together for long.

GO EASY

Perform steps 1–4 of the "Go" procedure. Move the skewer to different places. Notice where the red-dotted end of the magnet points with each trial.

GO FAR

Modify the "Go" procedure to build a portable, build-your-own compass that will work anywhere and read direction to within a 10° (±5° at any point on the 360° in a circle) margin of accuracy.

SHOW YOUR RESULTS:

For "Go Easy," display your apparatus and present a poster that shows how and why it works as a compass. For "Go," display your graph paper records, showing the orientation of the skewer and the direction the magnet pointed in each of your trials. For "Go Far," display your homemade compass and present experimental evidence to demonstrate that you achieved the 10° accuracy required.

Tips and Tricks

- If your magnet is taking a long time to settle, it's okay to slow it with your hand. Just let go before you determine where it is pointing.
- If your magnet swings back and forth slightly, draw the line in the middle that best represents its direction.
- Keep your setup at a distance from iron and steel objects. They can affect your results.

How Do Magnetic Fields Differ?

TALK IT OVER:

What are magnets? How do they work? Can you find a way to show the force that surrounds a magnet?

GET: _____

- Magnets, variety of sizes and shapes
- Glue or tape
- White paper plates, 1 for each magnet
- Outdoor place to work
- Face mask
- Goggles
- Rubber or heavy latex gloves
- Scissors
- Steel wool pad
- Salt shaker
- Spray adhesive

1. Glue or tape each magnet you want to test to the bottom of a white paper plate, like this:

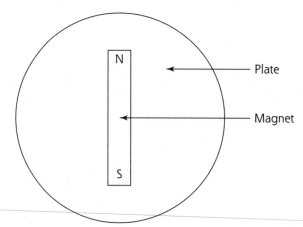

2. Outdoors, put on the safety goggles, face mask, and gloves.

3. Using scissors, cut tiny pieces from the steel wool pad into the salt shaker. Make the pieces as small as possible. Get the salt shaker about half full.

4. Shake steel wool pieces from the salt shaker onto a paper plate. Distribute the pieces as finely and evenly as you can. Watch as a pattern takes shape.

5. When you see the magnet's field clearly on the plate, stop shaking the steel pieces. Gently spray with spray adhesive to fix the steel wool pieces in place. You now have a permanent record of the magnet's field.

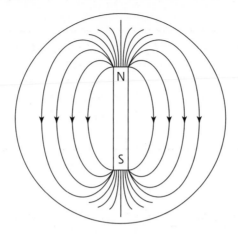

6. Repeat steps 4 and 5 for each magnet you want to study.

STAY SAFE:

Do not breathe in the tiny steel pieces or get them in your eyes or fingers. That's why the mask, goggles, and gloves are essential for this project. You can get all those supplies at a hardware store, and they are not expensive. Work outside in a well-ventilated area, and do not breathe in the spray adhesive. Wear your goggles and mask when you use the spray.

GO EASY

Make sure an adult works with you and that you follow all the safety procedures. Steel wool splinters in your fingers are no fun.

GO FAR

Use the "Go" procedure to show what happens when two magnets interact. Tape bar magnets to the bottoms of plates, turning the opposite poles toward or away from each other. Try to explain the differences in the magnetic fields you record this way.

You might also try capturing magnetic fields in gelatin. Ask an adult to help you make unflavored gelatin according to the directions on the package. Add steel wool pieces to the gelatin and put the mixture in a jam jar. Let it cool until it thickens slightly, but is not yet set. Then tape a magnet to the bottom of the jar and shake up the gelatin. Let it solidify in the refrigerator. With luck and a little practice, you may be able to capture magnetic fields in three dimensions this way.

MAGNETS

SHOW YOUR RESULTS:

For "Go Easy" and "Go," take photographs of your images or glue your plates directly to your display board. Draw pictures to show how the position of each magnet on the bottom of its plate relates to the field pattern you captured. Write a few sentences to explain what a magnetic field is. Describe how your magnetic fields vary in their shape, size, and strength.

Do the same for "Go Far," showing how the fields of two magnets differ depending on the orientation of the poles. If you capture magnetic fields in three dimensions, display your gelatin filled jars along with your project.

Tips and Tricks

- Spray the adhesive at a distance from the plates. Get too close and you'll push the steel pieces out of line.
- Don't use soapy steel wool pads for this project. Use plain steel wool pads that are available at hardware stores. Fine steel wool works best.

Are Two Magnets Twice as Strong as One?

TALK IT OVER:
What do magnets do? How do they work? How can you tell whether a magnet is strong or weak?

GET:

- 2 or more "button" magnets, ¾-inch diameter*
- A steel paper clip
- Pack of index cards

GO

1. Demonstrate the magnetic attraction of a magnet by using it to pick up a steel paper clip.
2. Demonstrate that the magnetic attraction can pass through a barrier by picking up the paper clip with a single index card between the magnet and the clip.

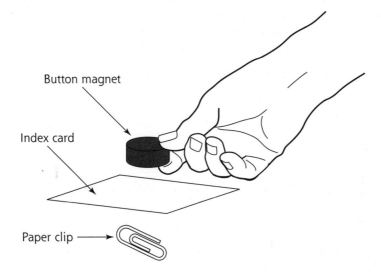

Button magnet

Index card

Paper clip

3. Add additional index cards between the magnet and the paper clip. Add them one at a time until the magnet can no longer hold the clip.

4. Count the number of index cards. This number is a measure of the strength of the magnet. (The greater the number of cards, the stronger the magnet.)

5. Put 2 button magnets together. (Notice that there is only one way they will hold.) Repeat steps 2–4. Record the number.

6. Continue testing with 3 or more magnets together if you wish. Record your measurement in each case.

STAY SAFE:

Magnets will not hurt you, but they can destroy data on computer hard drives, CDs, floppy disks, and cassette tapes. Keep magnets well away from such devices.

GO EASY

Compare your card count for 1 and 2 magnets only.

GO FAR

Get an assortment of bar, horseshoe, and button magnets to test and compare. Try testing other barriers to magnetic attraction such as glass, plastic, cloth, or water.

SHOW YOUR RESULTS:

Display your materials and let observers try the experiment for themselves. Put your numbers in a data table like this for "Go Easy" and "Go":

Number of Magnets	Strength (Number of Cards)
1	
2	
3 . . . and so on	

For "Go" and "Go Far," make a bar or line graph that compares the strength of 1, 2, or more magnets. For all projects, write a few sentences telling what your numbers mean and stating a conclusion. Use numbers to answer the following question: Are two magnets twice as strong as one?

Tips and Tricks

When testing your magnets, make sure the paper clip lines up squarely under the magnet each time you add a card and retest. If it's off to one side, you may get an inaccurate measurement.

How Does Distance Affect the Strength of a Magnet?

TALK IT OVER:

Magnets pull iron and steel objects toward them. Does it matter how far away from the object the magnet is? How can we measure the effect of distance on a magnet's strength?

GET:

- A compass with an easily read number scale (0–90 degrees between major compass points)*
- Sheet of graph paper (ruled in ¼-inch squares)
- Tape
- 1 or more small bar magnets*

GO

1. Place the compass so that the needle points toward your right. The needle should point exactly at one of the 0 (zero) marks, like this:

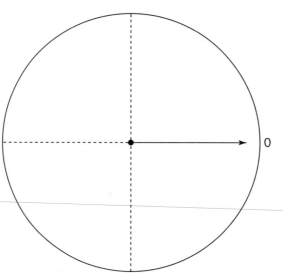

2. Place a piece of graph paper on the table between you and the compass. The lines on the graph paper should line up straight with the compass needle that still points to the right, like this:

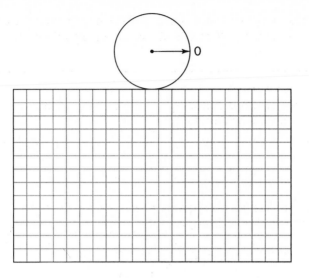

Not like this . . .

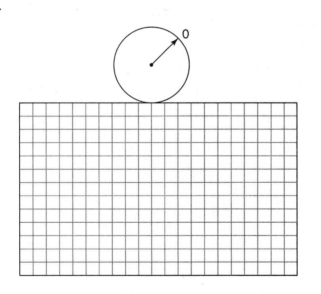

or this:

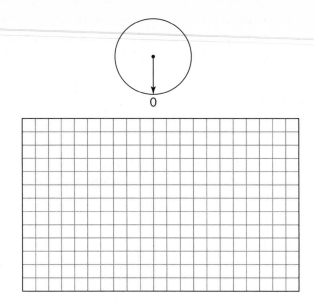

3. Tape down the graph paper and the compass so they cannot move.

4. Push an end of one of the bar magnets close to the compass. Make sure the compass needle moves toward you. If it moves away from you, turn the other end of the magnet toward the compass and try again.

5. Let the compass needle settle back to 0. Place the magnet with its end exactly 4 squares on the graph paper away from the compass. Read and record the number the compass needle moves to.

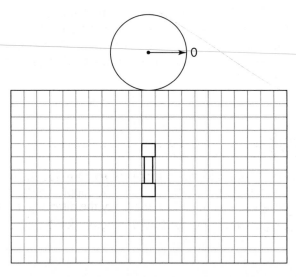

6. Move the bar back another 4 squares. Read and record the number the needle moves to. Keep doing this until you run out of graph paper squares.

STAY SAFE:

Magnets won't hurt you, but they will destroy the information stored on the magnetic strip on banking and credit cards. Keep your magnets and your wallet well away from each other.

GO EASY

The "Go" procedure will work for you.

GO FAR

You can hook small bar magnets together end-to-end. This allows you to test the distance effect using 2, 3, and 4 magnets. Create a mathematical statement from your data that relates the number of magnets to the distance effect.

SHOW YOUR RESULTS:

Put numbers in a data table like this for "Go" and "Go Easy":

Distance (in Squares)	Number on Compass Needle
4	
8	
12 . . . and so on	

For "Go Easy" and "Go," make bar or line graphs that show the relationship between distance and how far the compass needle moves. Display your materials so others can try the experiment for themselves.

For "Go Far," make separate data tables or add extra columns for the 2-, 3-, and 4-magnet combinations you test. Make line graphs that show the compass reading at different distances for 1, 2, 3, and 4 magnets. Use different color lines to show the result for each. Show your calculations and state any conclusions you drew about the relationship between numbers of magnets and distance.

Tips and Tricks

- If you can't find very small bar magnets like those shown here, you can substitute larger bar magnets you borrow from school or order from a scientific supply house. If your magnets are very large or very strong, however, you may need to modify the distances you test.
- You'll get some surprising results if you use button magnets for this experiment. Try it!

MAGNETS

Can a Toy Car Reveal the Strength of a Magnet?

TALK IT OVER:

What happens when the like poles of two magnets come close to each other? How could you use their interaction to move a toy car? Would the distance moved tell us anything about the strength of the magnet's force?

GET: _____

- Ruler (metric)
- Access to a photocopier
- Tape

- Small, plastic toy car
- Small bar magnets, 4 or more*

GO

1. Make a photocopy of the ruler. Tape it to the table.
2. Tape a small bar magnet to the top of a toy car.
3. Set the car at the 0 cm point on the ruled paper, like this:

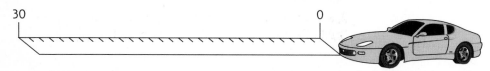

4. Bring an end of one small bar magnet near the magnet on the car. If the car moves toward you, reverse the ends of the magnet in your hand. You want the car to move *away* from you.
5. When you find the correct end, bring the magnet toward the car slowly, stopping when the car begins to move. Measure how far the car moved. Here's an example:

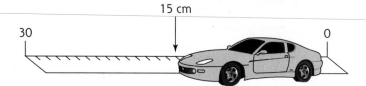

6. Repeat step 5 twice more. Average your results:

$$\frac{\text{Trial 1 distance} + \text{Trial 2 distance} + \text{Trial 3 distance}}{3} = \text{average distance}$$

7. Put 2 of the small bar magnets together to make a single, longer bar. Repeat steps 4–6.
8. Put 3 of the small bar magnets together to make a single, longer bar. Repeat steps 4–6.

STAY SAFE:

There's nothing dangerous in this experiment, but keep your magnets away from compasses, computers, and CDs. Magnets can erase data and distort compass readings.

GO EASY

You can do without measuring if you want. Just demonstrate how you can make the toy car move toward and away from you.

GO FAR:

The toy car moves away from the magnet because the same poles (north-north or south-south) of bar magnets repel each other. This *repulsive force* helps run magnetic levitation (*maglev* for short) trains. A repulsive magnetic force keeps the train suspended in the air above its track. Attractive and repulsive forces generated by electromagnets move the train forward. Because maglev trains don't touch the track, their friction is lower, so their energy consumption and noise levels are lower, too. Maglev trains are being used and evaluated in Japan and Germany. Find out about maglev trains and present information on them in your project. Invent a way to demonstrate the principles that keeps maglev trains suspended or moving forward. A good place to start is with the toy called a Levitron. Read more about it at www.levitron.com.

SHOW YOUR RESULTS:

Put distances in a data table like this for "Go":

Number of Magnets Tested (Length of Bar Magnet)	Distance Car Traveled			
	Trial 1	Trial 2	Trial 3	Average
1				
2				
3				

Make a bar graph of the average distances to answer the following question: Does a longer magnet make the car travel farther?

For "Go Easy," draw pictures to show what makes the car move toward or away from you.

For "Go Far," use models, data tables, and graphs to demonstrate how maglev trains work. Include information on maglev technology in your display.

Tips and Tricks

- Don't use a toy car made of steel for this experiment. It will be attracted to the magnet and spoil your measurements.
- When bringing your magnet near the car, make sure you are always in a straight line. Coming in at an angle will affect how far the car moves.

How Does Moisture Affect the Color of Soil?

TALK IT OVER:

What color is the soil in your yard, in the park, by the beach, or the lake? When it gets wet, does its color change? How? Why?

GET:

- Soil samples (take along small jars or ziptop bags, trowel or spoon, and a ruler)
- Marker
- Small baking dishes, 1 for each sample
- Tablespoon
- Cookie sheet
- Oven
- Camera (digital or film)

- Access to a computer or photocopier (to make black-and-white pictures)
- Grayscale (see "How to Make a Grayscale" in Part III)
- Water
- Measuring cup
- Spoon

GO

1. In jars or ziptop bags, collect small samples of soil from places near your home or school. (Be sure to ask permission.) Label each sample with a letter of the alphabet so you don't get mixed up. Keep good records. Write down where you got each sample and how deep you dug (use a ruler!).

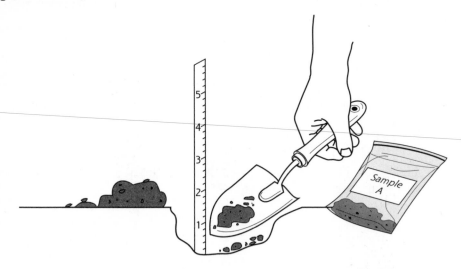

2. Using the marker, label small baking dishes with the same letters as your samples. Put 2 tablespoons of each sample in its labeled dish. Put the dishes on a cookie sheet.

3. Ask an adult to put the dishes in a warm oven (about 150°F). Leave them for several hours. This will bake the water out of your samples. Remove and let cool.

4. On a white piece of paper, write the letters of your samples. Put a teaspoon of each soil sample next to its letter.

5. Take a picture of the paper and samples. Use your computer to print a black-and-white copy, or make a black-and-white picture on a photocopier.

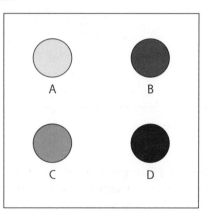

6. Compare the colors of the soils to the grayscale. Assign each soil a number from the grayscale that matches its color best.

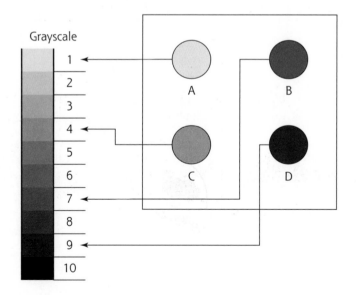

7. Add ¼ cup of water to each of the soil samples left in the baking dishes. Stir with a spoon to mix well.

8. Repeat steps 4–6. Did the soils change color? How? Did some soils change more than others?

STAY SAFE:

Let an adult use the oven for you, and don't touch the baking dishes until they cool. You might burn your fingers!

GO EASY

Compare potting soil and sand. Use the grayscale to compare their colors when dry and wet.

GO FAR

Online or in your library, find out about the Munsell system for describing the hue, value, and chroma (intensity) of colors. Use the system to compare and contrast soil samples taken from different locations or from different depths at the same location.

Expand your project by testing for different compounds in soil using soil test kits available from gardening centers and scientific supply houses. Does soil chemistry relate to color?

SHOW YOUR RESULTS:

Put numbers in a data table like this for "Go" and "Go Easy":

Soil Tested	Dry Grayscale Value (1–10)	Wet Grayscale Value (1–10)

For "Go," display your wet and dry samples, along with maps of where you collected them. For both "Go Easy" and "Go," make bar graphs that compare the grayscale values of wet and dry colors for each sample.

For "Go," subtract the dry grayscale value from the wet grayscale value to measure how much each sample changed and reveal which sample changed most. Try to explain any similarities and differences you find.

For "Go Far," display the Munsell system along with your samples and data tables. If you use a soil test kit, display your results. Try to explain the similarities and differences you observed.

How Does Porosity Vary in Rocks and Soils?

TALK IT OVER:

Rocks may look solid, but air actually fills millions of tiny spaces between rock particles. Soils have air spaces between their particles, too. The *porosity* of a rock or soil is the part of its volume that is *not* occupied by solid material. Porosity is important because it affects how much water underground rocks can hold. It also affects how well or how poorly soils hold the water needed to support plant growth.

GET:

- Rocks of different types
- Oven
- Cookie sheet
- Permanent marker
- Balance or kitchen scale (metric)
- Water
- Towel
- Soil samples
- Small baking dishes
- Measuring cups
- Cheesecloth

GO

1. Place your rock samples on a cookie sheet. Ask an adult to put them in a warm oven (150° F) for several hours. This will get them completely dry. Let them cool completely before you go on to step 2.

2. Write a number or letter on each sample with a permanent marker so you won't get them mixed up.

3. Weigh each of the rock samples on the balance or kitchen scale. Record the weight in grams.

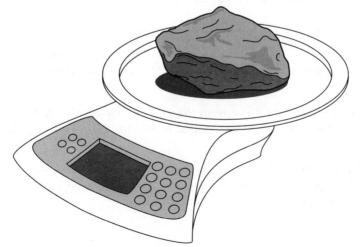

4. Soak the rock samples in water. Watch what happens. Make notes of your observations.

5. Let your rocks soak for several hours or overnight. Remove them from the water. Dry the rock's surface with a towel.

6. Weigh each rock on the kitchen scale. Calculate the grams of water that filled the pores in the rock:

$$\text{wet weight} - \text{dry weight} = \text{grams of water in pores}$$

7. Calculate the porosity of the rock:

$$\text{grams of water in pores} \div \text{dry weight} \times 100 = \text{percent porosity}$$

For example, if a 100-gram dry rock weighed 130 grams when full of water, the amount of water in its pores was 30 grams. Its porosity was $30 \div 100 = 0.30 \times 100 = 30\%$.

Note: Actually, porosity is defined by volume, not by weight. But since 1 gram of water occupies 1 milliliter of space, for convenience you'll use the two measures interchangeably.

8. Modify the procedure to test soil samples. Dry the soil in the oven in small baking dishes. Weigh the soil amounts. Flood with water and let sit for several hours. Pour the samples through cheesecloth to get excess water out and weigh again. Calculate the porosity of soils in the same way as you did for rocks.

STAY SAFE:

Stay away from the hot oven. Let an adult dry your samples for you. Don't work with the rock and soil samples until they cool. If you collect soil samples, make sure you ask the owner's permission to dig.

GO EASY

Test only rocks. Leave soil testing for next year.

GO FAR

Experts estimate the porosity of rocks and soils as follows:

Material	Porosity (percent)
Soil	55
Gravel and sand	20–50
Clay	50–70
Sandstone	5–30
Limestone	10–30
Fractured igneous rocks	10–40

Accept these estimates as your hypotheses and conduct experiments to test them.

To learn more, find out about *specific retention*. In groundwater, it is the volume of water that will not flow through rock because it is held by surface tension on the rock's particles. The volume that can flow through freely is *specific yield*. It is always less than porosity. Find out how tightly packed and loosely packed rocks and soils differ in these properties; then design experiments to measure them.

SHOW YOUR RESULTS:

Put your measurements and calculations in a table like this:

Rock/Soil	Dry Weight	Wet Weight	Wet − Dry	Porosity (in Percent)
Rock 1				
Rock 2				
Soil A . . . and so on				

Make bar graphs that show how the porosities of your samples differ.

For "Go Far," compare each calculated porosity with its hypothesis. If the hypothesis is not confirmed, try to explain why. If you design experiments to measure specific retention and specific yield, make tables and graphs similar to those suggested for "Go."

Tips and Tricks

- Does porosity relate to the size of the particles? Here's a quick way to find out. Fill a measuring cup to the 1-cup mark with large beads. Add water until its level matches the top of the beads. Measure the amount of water you added. Now repeat the experiment, but this time use tiny beads. Try to explain any similarities or differences you find.

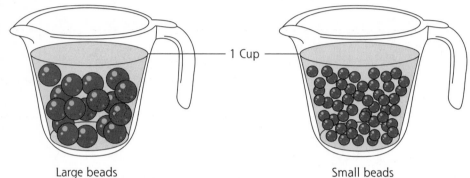

Large beads   Small beads

- Specific yield is also called *permeability*. To demonstrate how it can differ in soils, fill 2 glass, graduated cylinders to the 100-milliliter mark with sand (in one) and potting soil (in the other). Tap down lightly. Then add 20 ml of water to both. Use the color change to find how far down the column the water travels. What does this tell you about permeability differences?

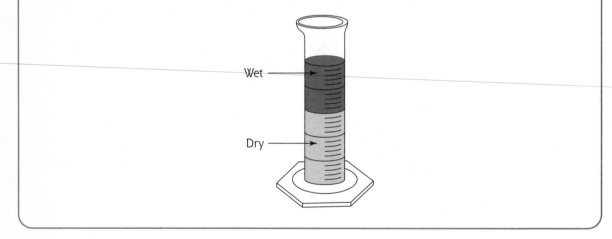

Wet

Dry

How Compact Are the Soils Near Your Home and School?

TALK IT OVER:

What's in soil? It's part soil particles, part water, and part air. Healthy soils that support good plant growth have ample air spaces in them. Water moves through them easily. Soils that get too packed down don't drain well. The compression of soil particles is called *compaction*. Heavy equipment and construction work compress soils. Soils that have a lot of clay in them are also very compact. You can measure the compaction of soils in your area. Perhaps you can relate what you measure to how well—or how poorly—plants grow in the places you study.

GET:

- Metal knitting needle, size 7 or smaller
- Small spool
- Ruler (metric)
- Access to a photocopier
- Scissors
- Transparent tape
- Permission to test soils in the sites you choose

GO

1. Make sure the knitting needle fits through the spool, like this:

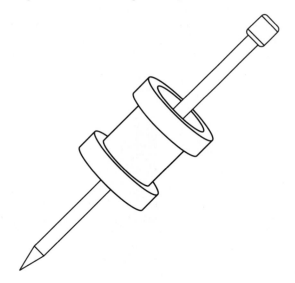

2. Make a photocopy of the ruler (centimeter side). Cut out the thin strip of marks and numbers.

3. Set the spool on a table. Put the knitting needle, point side down, in the spool. Tape the ruler strip to the knitting needle, with the 0 at the top edge of the spool. Tape the strip very securely so that it will hold when you push the needle into the ground.

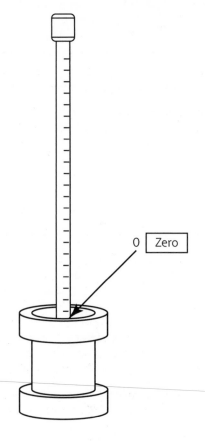

0 | Zero

4. To measure compaction, place the spool and knitting needle on the soil surface. Push down hard. The top of the spool will show you how far the needle went into the soil. The *farther* it goes, the *less* compaction.

5. Take compaction measurements at different sites near your home and school. (Be sure to ask permission.) Observe the plants that grow in each site you measure. Can you relate compaction to plant growth?

STAY SAFE:

Be careful with the point of the knitting needle. It is not sharp, but it could poke you or someone else.

GO EASY

The "Go" procedure will work for you.

GO FAR

Water has a big effect on how far soils compact when pressed—as they are, for example, when a tractor or mower runs over them. Devise a way to measure the effects of water on compaction. Use your experimental design to compare soil samples taken from sites in your area.

Surface compaction and *subsoil* compaction are different. Find out about them. Then design and carry out experiments that will let you compare and contrast their mechanisms and effects.

SHOW YOUR RESULTS:

You can keep track of your measurements and observations using a table like this:

Test Site	Location of Site	Compaction Measurement (cm)	Relative Compaction (Circle One)	Plants I Observed at This Site
A			High Medium Low	
B			High Medium Low	
C . . . and so on			High Medium Low	

Make bar graphs to compare compaction at the different sites. (Remember, the greater the measurement, the less compact the soil—and the better for plant life.) You might want to take photographs or draw pictures of your test sites to relate plant growth to compaction.

For "Go Far," make data tables and graphs to match the experiments you design and conduct. Include in your display information about the different forms of compaction and how water and mechanical action affect them.

Tips and Tricks

- If you test many soils that are very wet or very compact, your measuring strip may pull loose. Take tape and extra photocopied strips into the field with you so you can make repairs at your test sites if you need to.
- If you live in an agricultural area, ask a farmer about the impact of soil compaction on crop yields. Find out what is done to reduce or prevent it.

Does the Temperature Underground Vary as Much as the Surface Temperature Does?

TALK IT OVER:

The soil below the earth's surface is home to many living things. Some insects live underground for all or part of their life cycles. Some larger animals, such as moles and earthworms, live underground all the time. Others, such as the prairie dog, spend part of their time on the surface and part in a burrow they dig below ground. What might be some of the advantages of living below ground? Are animals cooler or warmer below ground?

GET:

- Permission to dig small holes in a few spots in the ground
- Small shovel or trowel
- Ruler
- Craft sticks and marker
- Digital instant-read thermometer*

GO

1. Select your sites with care. Ideally, you want to investigate some places that are sunny and warm and others that are shaded and cool.

2. Plan ahead for this project. The longer you collect data (over weeks, even months), the better your project will be.

3. At each site you want to study, dig a small hole or "burrow" in the ground. Don't dig it straight down, like this:

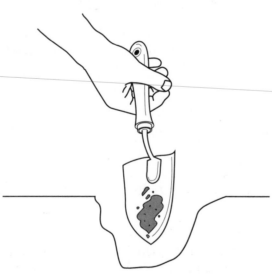

Dig it at an angle, like this:

4. Write a name for your site on a craft stick and push the stick into the ground near the burrow you have dug. With luck, it will stay in place and mark your study site for as long as you continue to collect data.

5. Hold the thermometer in the air near your burrow. Read and record the air temperature.

6. Place the thermometer on the ground near your burrow. Read and record the surface temperature.

7. Put the thermometer into the burrow. Leave it for a few seconds, then pull it out quickly and read it immediately (before the surface air temperature has time to change it). Record.

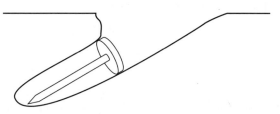

8. Repeat steps 3–7 for each site you study. Return daily, for as long as you can, to collect as much data as you can.

STAY SAFE:

Don't trespass on anyone's land. Don't dig holes where people might step into them. Don't put a thermometer into a burrow an animal has dug. The animal might still be inside!

GO EASY

Use the "Go" procedure to study a warm, sunny spot and a cool, shaded spot.

GO FAR

Make some telephone calls to see whether you can borrow a *pyranometer* from a commercial or college laboratory. With a pyranometer, you can measure *albedo,* which is the amount of light reflected from a surface. Albedo can affect both surface and air temperatures. Does it affect underground temperatures? Design and conduct a study that will let you relate albedo to your air, surface, and underground temperature data.

SHOW YOUR RESULTS:

For each site you study, make a data table like this:

Site_____ Location _____ Description_____				
Date	Time	Air Temperature (°C)	Surface Temperature (°C)	Underground Temperature (°C)

For each site, make a line graph with temperature on the vertical axis and time on the horizontal axis. Use different color lines for air, surface, and underground temperatures. The shapes of the lines should tell you something about how temperatures vary and where they vary most.

For "Go Far," make similar data tables and graphs to relate albedo to air, surface, and underground temperatures.

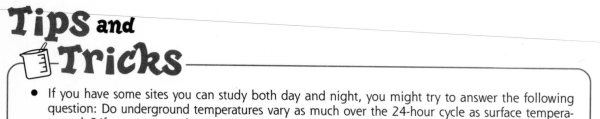

Tips and Tricks

- If you have some sites you can study both day and night, you might try to answer the following question: Do underground temperatures vary as much over the 24-hour cycle as surface temperatures do? If you can extend your project over several months, try to assess seasonal variations as well.
- Make sure you keep with you a fresh battery for your instant read, digital thermometer. You don't want to run low when you are in the field taking temperatures.

What Tests Can You Use to Identify Minerals?

TALK IT OVER:

Minerals are chemicals that are present in rocks and soil. They have a uniform chemical composition and a definite crystalline structure. Some are made of a single element, such as gold. Others are compounds of two of more elements. Magnetite is a good example. It is made of iron and oxygen.

If you had a mineral that you couldn't identify, what observations and tests could you use to find its name?

GET:

- Several samples of unknown minerals*
- Bright light
- Magnifying glass
- Penny
- Steel nail
- Glass plate (from a picture frame is fine)
- 1 bathroom tile

- Kitchen scale or balance (metric)
- Small yogurt container, empty, washed and dried
- Small bowl
- Water
- Measuring cup (metric)

GO

Here I will suggest four properties you can test for and use to distinguish minerals: *luster, hardness* (on the Mohs scale), *streak color,* and *specific gravity.* There are many others you may want to learn about and use in your project, but these will get you started.

- **Luster:** Observe each sample carefully under a bright light, using a magnifying glass or hand lens. Look at its texture and surface appearance. Decide which of the following descriptions fits it best:
    - Metallic (shiny like a metal)
    - Shiny (like a diamond)
    - Glassy
    - Resinous (looks like sap, gum, pitch, or tar)
    - Pearly
    - Oily or greasy
    - Silky (appears to have fibers like a woven fabric)
- **Hardness:** Next, determine how hard or soft the mineral is, using the Mohs scale of hardness.

175

Mohs Scale of Hardness

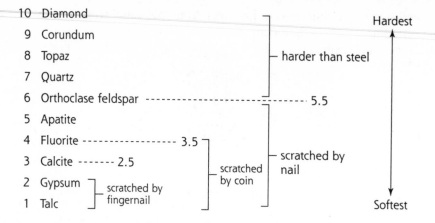

10 Diamond — Hardest

9 Corundum

8 Topaz — harder than steel

7 Quartz

6 Orthoclase feldspar ------------------------ 5.5

5 Apatite

4 Fluorite ---------------- 3.5 — scratched by nail

3 Calcite ------- 2.5 — scratched by coin

2 Gypsum — scratched by fingernail

1 Talc — Softest

- This scale is relative. You assign a number to a mineral by seeing what scratches what. To get the *range* of hardness for a sample do this:

  1. Try scratching it with your fingernail. If you can, the Mohs scale hardness value is 2.5 or *less*.

  2. Try scratching with a penny. If you can, the value is 3.5 or *less*.

  3. Try scratching with a steel nail. If you can, the value is 5.5 or *less*.

  4. See whether the mineral will scratch glass. If it will, the Mohs value is 6 *or more*.

- **Streak color:** Use the back of a bathroom tile as your streak plate. Rub the mineral across it and examine the color of the streak.

- **Specific gravity:** To find a mineral's specific gravity (or its density, the ratio of its mass to its volume), do this:

  1. Weigh the mineral on the balance or kitchen scale. Record the weight in grams.

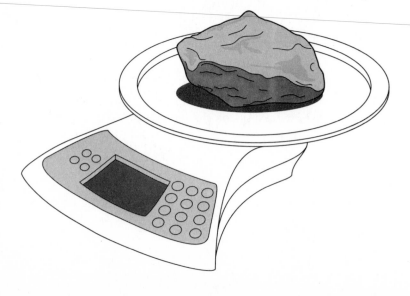

2. Set the small yogurt container in the bowl. Fill the yogurt container with water to the brim, but don't let it run over.

3. Carefully drop the mineral into the water. Water will spill from the yogurt container into the bowl.

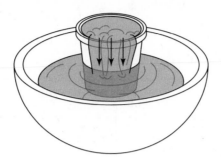

4. When water stops spilling over, remove the container from the bowl. Pour the water from the bowl into the measuring cup. Measure and record the amount of water in milliliters. This equals the volume of the mineral.

5. The specific gravity of the mineral is its weight in grams divided by its volume in milliliters. (*Note:* Specific gravity is defined in relation to the density of water, which is 1g/1ml. Therefore, it has no units.) In the example, the specific gravity is 2.5 times that of water, or 2.5g/ml. Use the calculator to find the specific gravity of each mineral you test. For example, if the weight of a sample is 25 grams and its volume is 10 milliliters, its specific gravity is 25 ÷ 10 = 2.5.

Some common minerals and their characteristics for these properties are shown in this table:

Mineral	Luster	Hardness on the Mohs Scale	Streak	Specific Gravity
Apatite	Glassy	5	White	3.2
Azurite	Glassy	3.5	Blue	3.8
Biotite	Pearly	2.5	White	3.1
Calcite	Glassy	3	White	2.7
Feldspar	Pearly	6	White	2.7
Fluorite	Glassy	4	White	3.2
Galena	Metallic	2.5	Black or gray	7.5
Gypsum	Pearly	2	White	2.3
Hematite	Metallic	6.5	Brown	5.3
Limonite	Silky	3	Brownish yellow	4.7
Magnetite	Metallic	5.5	Black	5.2
Nepheline	Greasy	6	White	2.6
Quartz	Glassy	7	White	2.7
Sphalerite	Shiny (like a diamond)	3.5	White	4.0
Sulfur	Resinous	2	White	2.1
Talc	Pearly	1	White	2.8

STAY SAFE:

Be careful of the edges on the glass plate. They can scratch you.

GO EASY

Test your samples for luster, hardness, and streak color. Leave specific gravity for next year.

GO FAR

Some other characteristics of minerals that you may incorporate into your project are tenacity, color, magnetism, crystal habit, chatoyancy, asterism, piezoelectricity, cleavage, parting, fracture, fluorescence, and phosphorescence. About 4,000 different minerals have been named and described, and new ones are added to the catalog every year. You can't study them all, but you can use your science project to get a start.

SHOW YOUR RESULTS:

Put your data in a table like the one above, but don't put in the names of the minerals unless you know them for sure. Label your specimens A, B, C, and so on. Describe and display them for your project. You may want to make a bar graph to compare the hardness or specific gravity of some of your samples.

Tips and Tricks

- You can improve your hardness estimates by rubbing your samples against each other. If one scratches the other, it's harder.
- You can get reasonable specific gravity estimates with a kitchen scale and a metric measuring cup, but you'll do better with a laboratory balance and a graduated cylinder. Your science teacher might be able to lend you these tools for a short time.

What Do Yeast Eat . . . and How Can You Tell?

TALK IT OVER:

Those brown granules in a packet or jar of baking yeast may look dead, but they actually contain millions of microscopic, living yeast cells that eat, grow, and make more yeast cells when conditions are right. You can't see them eating, but you can see evidence that they do.

GET:

- 2 empty plastic lemons or limes
  (with dropper inserts and screw caps)
- Small fishing weights
- Measuring cup
- Active dry yeast
- Measuring spoons

- Spoon
- Molasses
- Marker
- Deep pot
- Warm water
- Stopwatch (optional, for "Go Far")

GO

1. Remove the caps and dropper inserts from the plastic fruits. Wash and rinse them well inside and out.

2. Count out enough fishing weights to fill each fruit about ¼ full. Put the same number and size of weights in each fruit.

3. Fill the measuring cup with warm (not hot) water to the 1-cup mark. Add a teaspoon of active dry yeast. Stir with a spoon until all the yeast grains dissolve.

1 Cup

4. Carefully pour the yeast-and-water mixture into 1 of the fruits. Fill it all the way to the top. Put on the dropper insert and screw cap.

5. Add 1 teaspoon of molasses to the yeast-water mixture that is still in the measuring cup. Stir well.

6. Fill the other plastic fruit with the yeast-water-molasses mixture. Put on the dropper insert and cap. With the marker, write a big "M" on the fruit, so you know it has molasses in it.

7. Set both fruits in the pot. Add enough warm (not hot) water to cover the fruits completely.

8. Working underwater, remove the caps (but not the dropper inserts) from both fruits.

9. Within 10–20 minutes you should see something start to happen. Describe the differences you see and try to explain them.

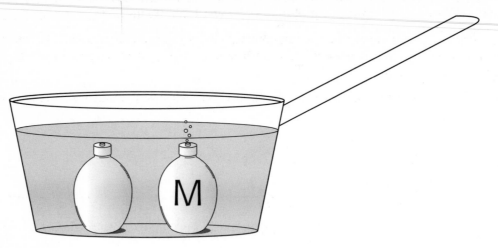

10. Determine what the yeast cells are using for food. How do you know?

STAY SAFE:

Avoid tap water that is too hot. You'll burn your fingers and kill your yeast.

GO EASY

Mix 1 teaspoon of dry yeast into each of 2 cups of warm water. Add 1 teaspoon of molasses to 1 cup but not to the other. Leave both for 30 minutes in a warm place. What differences do you see?

GO FAR

Set up the experiment as in "Go," but use a stopwatch and count the number of bubbles that rise from each fruit each minute. Keep counting and recording minute-by-minute until the bubbles stop. What does the change in the number of bubbles per minute tell you about how the yeast population is growing? (**Hint:** The more yeast cells there are, the more food they consume.)

Use the bubble-counting method to measure and compare yeast growth rates when you test

- Equal amounts of different yeast foods such as sugar, honey, corn syrup, or jelly
- Different amounts of the same food (such as ¼, ½, and 1 teaspoon of molasses added to equal amounts of water)
- The effects of temperature by submerging your filled fruits in hot, warm, and cold water
- How other substances added to the mixture (such as vinegar, lemon juice, salt, or baking soda) affect yeast growth

SHOW YOUR RESULTS:

For "Go Easy," report your observations like this: In the cup without molasses, I saw _____.
In the cup with molasses, I saw _____. I think this means that _____.

For "Go," draw diagrams of your setups and observations. Write a few sentences telling what you saw and explaining what you think caused it. Put fresh setups in your project display so others can see for themselves what happens.

For "Go Far," make a line graph showing the number of bubbles you counted each minute under the different conditions you tested.

Tips and Tricks

If you use too few fishing weights, your plastic fruits may start to float after a while. If that happens, repeat the experiment, using more weights.

Does Garlic Prevent Microbial Growth?

TALK IT OVER:

Individual *microbes* are tiny living things too small for us to see, but if millions of them live and multiply on some food, you can see their *colonies.* That's what we see when fruit rots and bread molds. How can you find out whether garlic inhibits the growth of microbes?

GET:

- 8 or more small canning jars with lids
- Access to a dishwasher
- Paper towels
- Marker or labels
- Unflavored gelatin, 1 box (4 packets)
- Sugar
- Canned chicken broth
- Tap water
- Measuring cup
- Measuring spoons
- Cooking pot
- Garlic powder
- Funnel
- Book
- 1 gallon *distilled* water (available in the laundry products section of the supermarket)
- Cotton swabs
- Box
- Drawing materials or camera
- Magnifying glass or hand lens

GO

1. Wash the jars and lids in a dishwasher. Remove them immediately after the dry cycle and turn them upside down on the paper towels. You want to prevent microbes from the air from entering your jars as much as you can.

2. Label three jars "garlic." Label another three "no garlic." Label one jar "garlic control." Label another jar "no garlic control."

3. Decide on three sources of microbes you would like to study. You might try soil, sour milk, the floor, a doorknob, or inside your nose or mouth.

4. Make two labels for each source you choose. Put one of each label on a "garlic" jar. Put the other of each label on a "no garlic jar."

5. Have an adult do the cooking for you. Ask the adult to prepare two batches of "microbe food" using this recipe:

    a. In a clean pot, mix 2 packets of unflavored gelatin and 1 teaspoon of sugar with ½ cup canned chicken broth and ¾ cup water. This makes 1 batch of microbe food. Make a second batch using the same recipe, but add 1 teaspoon of garlic powder.

    b. On medium heat, bring to a boil, stirring constantly until the gelatin dissolves completely.

    c. For each batch, pour the microbe food through the funnel into the jars. Put approximately equal amounts into four jars. (You will make eight jars in all, four from each batch of microbe food. Make sure the labels match the food formulas.)

d. Carefully turn the jars on their sides and place their tops on a book, so the microbe food solidifies at an angle like this:

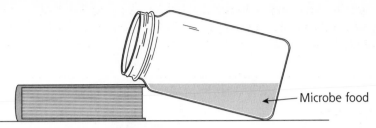

e. Let the microbe food cool and harden.

6. After the microbe food has set, dampen a cotton swab with a little distilled water, then rub it over your first microbe source. Sweep the swab *gently* over the surface of the microbe food in the appropriately labeled jars, like this:

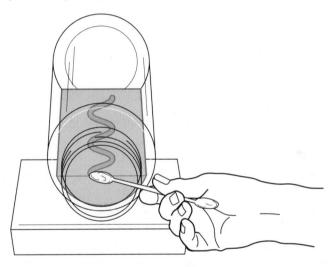

Do not push hard or break the surface of the gelatin.

7. Repeat with the two other microbe sources, using clean swabs each time. Make sure the microbe source you use matches the labels on the jars.

8. For the jars labeled "control," dampen the swabs with distilled water only. Do not use a microbe source, but move the swab over the surface of the microbe food in the same manner.

9. Put the lids on the jars tightly. Put the jars in the box, with the book still under them so the gelatin remains at a slant. Put the box in a warm place, with the jars out of direct sunlight.

10. Observe the surface of the microbe food daily, looking through the glass jar. A magnifying glass or hand lens may help you see better. Do not open the jars. Make sketches or take photographs each time you observe. Take notes describing the similarities and differences you notice.

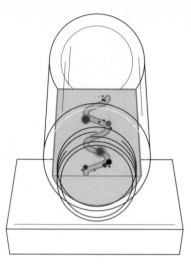

STAY SAFE:

- Cooking the microbe food is an adult job. Don't try to do it yourself.
- Don't keep your experiment in the kitchen or near where food is prepared or eaten. If a jar breaks, you might get microbes in your food.
- Once you seal your jars, don't ever open them again. Dangerous microbes could grow inside. Dispose of your jars in a safe manner. Do not display your jars with your project. Show your photographs or drawings instead.

GO EASY

The "Go" procedure will work for you. Make sure you understand how to keep this experiment safe. Stay away from the stove and hot microbe food. Let an adult do that part for you.

GO FAR

Use the "Go" procedure to see whether the amount of garlic in the microbe food makes a difference. Or you might compare fresh garlic, garlic powder, and ground-up garlic tablets. Test the claims that onions, tea tree oil, and cinnamon are effective microbe killers. You might also study the effects of refrigeration on microbe growth.

SHOW YOUR RESULTS:

Your photographs and sketches will show if there are any differences between the "garlic" and "no garlic" jars. Pictures of your "control" jars are just as important. If you get much growth in them, microbes from the air have contaminated all your jars, so you won't be able to say much about the effects of garlic. You will, however, have demonstrated how microbes are *everywhere* around us, even if we don't see them.

Tips and Tricks

- Don't let your microbes continue to grow for too long. Microbe colonies will eventually overgrow the surfaces of the food. The warmer the place, the sooner this happens.
- Don't even think about opening and cleaning the jars for future use. Discard them after your experiment ends. As you observe your results, you'll see why!

How Does a Salt Concentration Affect the Hatching of Brine Shrimp Eggs?

TALK IT OVER:

Brine shrimp are tiny crustaceans. (*Crustaceans* are animals that have a hard shell and many jointed legs.) They are relatives of crabs, lobsters, and crayfish. Their eggs are very hardy. They can last for years as dry cysts and then hatch within a day or two into brine shrimp *larvae*. Within a week, they can go through several stages of development, becoming mature brine shrimp. Brine shrimp normally live in salt water. How can you find out which salt concentration is best for hatching them?

GET:

- 4 wide-mouthed quart jars, with lids
- Labels and pen
- Measuring cup
- 1 gallon *distilled* water (available in the laundry products aisle of the supermarket)
- Sea salt
- Measuring spoon set

- Brine shrimp eggs*
- Desk lamp
- Magnifying glass
- Black paper
- Clear glass plate or bowl
- Packet of dry yeast, aquarium, and aerator (optional, for "Go Far")

GO

1. Label the jars 1, 2, 3, and 4.
2. Add 3 cups of distilled water to each jar.
3. To jar 1, add 1 tablespoon of sea salt. To jar 2, add 2 tablespoons. To jar 3, add 3 tablespoons. Add no sea salt to jar 4.
4. Put the lids on the jars and shake them well to dissolve the salt completely.
5. Remove the lids. Add ⅛ teaspoon of brine shrimp eggs to each jar. Swirl gently to mix.
6. Put the jars in a warm, *lighted* place for 24 to 48 hours (under a desk lamp works fine).
7. Every few hours, gently swirl the water in the jars to keep the water oxygenated and to mix the contents. Swirl all jars equally.
8. Observe frequently, using the magnifying glass, and keep notes in your log book of what you see in the jars.

9. After about 48 hours, swirl the jars to mix the contents thoroughly. Place the clear glass plate or bowl on the black paper and shine the desk lamp on it. Then take 1 teaspoon of water from jar 1 and place it on the glass. Use the magnifying glass to find and count brine shrimp larvae. They look like this:

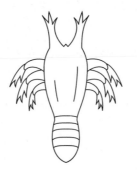

10. Count the number of live brine shrimp larvae you see in 1 teaspoon of water from jar 1. Repeat 3 times, with 3 different 1-teaspoon samples. Record the counts and average them, like this:

$$\frac{\text{number in Sample 1} + \text{number in Sample 2} + \text{number in Sample 3}}{3} = \text{average number in 1 tsp}$$

11. Repeat steps 9 and 10 with 1-teaspoon samples of water from each of the other jars.

STAY SAFE:

Nothing in this project can hurt you, but clean hands are always a good idea.

GO EASY

The "Go" procedure will work for you. Get an adult's help with the measuring, counting, and calculating.

GO FAR

There are many experiments you can design and carry out with brine shrimp eggs, larvae, and adults. You might, for example, modify the "Go" procedure to see how other salt concentrations, temperatures, or light/dark conditions affect the hatching rate.

It's easy to raise brine shrimp larvae to the adult stage. You'll need a small aquarium and an aerator, plus dry yeast for food. (You'll find many books and Web sites that tell you how to keep brine shrimp.) You might use adult brine shrimp to investigate the effects of pollutants such as oil or acid rain. Or you can observe and measure their responses to environment stimuli such as light, heat, or even magnetism.

MICROSCOPIC LIFE

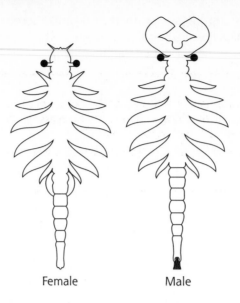

Female   Male

SHOW YOUR RESULTS:

Put numbers and observations in tables like this for "Go" and "Go Easy:"

Date _____ Time: _____		
Jar	**Observations**	**Hatching Rate (Number of Larvae in 1 tsp.)**
1		Sample 1: Sample 2: Sample 3: Average:
2		Sample 1: Sample 2: Sample 3: Average:
3 . . . and so on		

Make a bar graph of the number of larvae in an average 1-teaspoon sample taken from each jar. Explain how the number of larvae relates to the solutions they hatched in.

For "Go Far," make tables and graphs to match the experiments you designed. You might want to include a diagram of the brine shrimp life cycle with your project display.

Tips and Tricks

- Newly hatched brine shrimp larvae are only about 0.25mm (0.01 inch) long, so you'll have to look closely when counting them through a magnifying glass. You'll have an easier time if you can borrow a dissecting microscope from your school.
- Adult brine shrimp are a little bigger (10–15 mm, which is about ½ inch), so they are much easier to see.

What Makes the Best Compost Pile?

TALK IT OVER:

One way of recycling kitchen waste is to make compost and use it in the garden. What is compost? How is it made? How does composting recycle waste?

GET:

- 6 ziptop, plastic bags, sandwich size
- Labels and pen
- 6 plastic straws
- Digital instant-read thermometer*
- Scissors
- Tape

- Lettuce
- Knife
- Newspaper
- Kitchen scale
- Water
- Measuring spoons

1. Label the bags 1, 2, 3, 4, 5, and 6.

2. Make sure the probe of the thermometer fits through the straws. Cut the straws so they are about 2 cm (1 inch) shorter than the thermometer probe, like this:

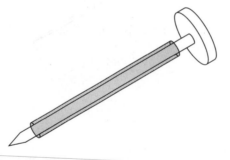

3. Tape 1 straw inside each bag, so that about 1 cm sticks out above the top of the bag, like this:

4. Ask an adult to chop the lettuce into very small pieces—the smaller, the better. Use scissors to cut the newspaper into tiny pieces.

5. On the kitchen scale, weigh lettuce and newspaper, and add them to the bags as indicated in this chart:

Bag Number	Newspaper in Grams (Ounces)	Lettuce in Grams (Ounces)
1	0	0
2	200 (8)	0 (0)
3	0 (0)	200 (8)
4	50 (2)	150 (6)
5	100 (4)	100 (4)
6	150 (6)	50 (2)

In bags 4–6, mix the lettuce and newspaper evenly inside the bag.

6. Add a tablespoon of water to each bag. Check to make sure the bottoms of the straws extend into the bag's contents but do not touch the bottom of the bag:

7. Seal the ziptop from both edges toward the straw. Tape around the outside of the straw to seal the bag shut.

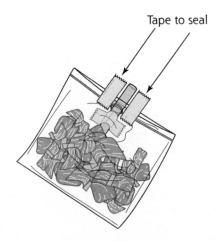

Tape to seal

8. Set the bags in a warm, dark place.

9. Every day for several days, measure and record the temperature of the air near the bags. Also record the temperature inside the bags, inserting the thermometer's probe through the straws. Also make notes about what you see in the bag.

10. When the experiment ends, throw the bags away without opening them.

STAY SAFE:

Don't cut the lettuce yourself. Ask an adult to do it for you. Don't open the bags once they are sealed. The contents may contain dangerous microbes. Don't try this experiment if you have mold allergies. Wash your hands before and after handling the bags.

GO EASY

Set up only bags 1–4. Ask an adult to help you with weighing and taking temperatures inside the bags.

GO FAR

"Go" offers a basic procedure you can use to investigate composting. Modify it to investigate factors you think may affect the speed of the decay process. You might, for example, find out whether temperature, the size of the pieces, or light/dark conditions affect the speed of the breakdown. You might also experiment with other materials such as grass clippings, potato peels, apple cores, cardboard, wood shavings, sawdust, straw, or leaves. Or you might assess whether some of the commercial products that are sold to speed up the composting process actually work.

SHOW YOUR RESULTS:

For "Go Easy, put your data in a table like this:

	Date:_____ Time: _____ Air Temp: _____		Date:_____ Time:_____ Air Temp: ____		Date:_____ Time:_____ Air Temp: _____	
Bag	Observations	Temperature	Observations	Temperature	Observations	Temperature
1						
2						
3						
4						

Pick a day when you noticed temperature differences among the bags. Make a bar graph that shows the difference. In your report, explain how bag 1 serves as a control. Tell what the temperature difference in other bags reveals about the composting process.

For "Go," add rows for bags 5 and 6 to your data table. Make a line graph of temperatures (on the vertical axis) by time (on the horizontal axis). Use lines of different colors to represent temperatures inside the individual bags. If you see differences in bags 4–6, what explains them? Do your results tell you anything about the best mixture of composting materials?

For "Go Far," modify the data table to fit your experimental design. Make line graphs that help you answer the question you chose to investigate.

Tips and Tricks

- Old, slightly stale lettuce works best.
- Don't use color print or glossy magazine sections from the newspaper. Use plain, black-and-white printed pages.
- If you don't get good results with this experiment, try again, adding more or less water. The moisture level inside the bag is important.
- Do not put meat, milk, or animal fats or foods in the bags. You won't like the results.

Do Hand Soaps and Sanitizers Prevent the Growth of Bread Mold?

TALK IT OVER:

Sometimes you have to throw your bread out. It gets mold growing on it. Some bread molds look green. Some are black, white, or orange. You can use bread molds as a convenient way to test how well hand sanitizers and soaps work against microscopic life forms like molds.

GET: _____

- 8 ziptop plastic bags, sandwich size
- Labels and pen
- Latex gloves
- 4 slices of bread
- Toaster
- Knife
- Cookie sheet
- Spray bottle of water
- 1 soap and 1 hand sanitizer to test
- Measuring teaspoon
- Camera or drawing materials

GO

1. Label the bags as shown in the table:

Bag Number	Bread	Treatment
1	Not toasted	None
2	Not toasted	Water spray only
3	Not toasted	Soap spray
4	Not toasted	Hand sanitizer spray
5	Toasted	None
6	Toasted	Water spray only
7	Toasted	Soap spray
8	Toasted	Hand sanitizer spray

2. Wear the gloves as you set up this experiment. Toast two of the bread slices.

3. Get an adult to cut all the bread slices in half for you, like this:

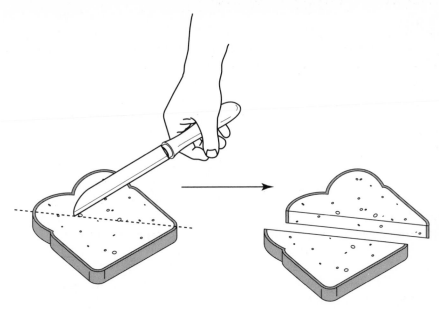

You have four pieces that are toasted and four pieces that are not toasted. Put them on the cookie sheet.

4. Put a piece that is not toasted in bag 1. Seal. Put a toasted piece in bag 5 and seal.

5. Put water in the spray bottle. Spray an untoasted and a toasted piece *lightly* with a fine mist of water. Put them in bags 2 and 6. Seal the bags.

6. Add 1 teaspoon of the hand soap to the water in the spray bottle. Shake to mix thoroughly. Spray as you did in step 5 to add pieces to bags 3 and 7.

7. Empty the spray bottle and rinse it several times. Add fresh water and 1 teaspoon of hand sanitizer. Shake to mix thoroughly. Spray as you did in step 5 to make the last 2 slices for bags 4 and 8.

8. Put all the bags, sprayed side up, on the cookie sheet. Place them in a warm, dark place. Every day, observe the bread in the bags. Take careful notes. If you see mold colonies (colored or fuzzy circles) on the bread, count them. Take or draw pictures of what you see in the bags.

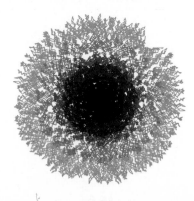

STAY SAFE:

Do not open the bags after the experiment begins and discard them safely when it is over. Dangerous microbes are not likely to grow inside the bags, but it is possible.

GO EASY

Set up only bags 1–4, using only untoasted bread.

GO FAR

Extend your project by investigating other variables that could affect the kinds of molds that grow on the bread and their growth rate. You might try varying temperature, humidity, light/dark, or the kind of container the bread is kept in. Do some research to identify the kinds of *fungi* (the scientific name for molds) that commonly grow on bread, and learn to identify them. If you have a dissecting microscope—or if you can borrow one from you school—you can examine the molds on your bread and draw pictures of their structure. One common one, called *Rhizopus*, looks like this:

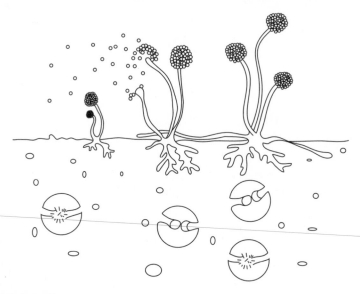

SHOW YOUR RESULTS:

Put your data in a table like this for "Go Easy":

Bag Number	Day 1 Observations	Day 1 Colony Count	Day 2 Observations	Day 2 Colony Count	Day 3 Observations	Day 3 Colony Count	And So On . . .
1							
2							
3							
4							

For "Go," add rows for bags 5–8. For both "Go" and "Go Easy," make bar graphs that compare colony counts in the bags each day. Relate mold growth to the treatment the bread received, using bags 1 and 5 as your *controls,* or basis for comparison.

For "Go Far," use similar data tables and make similar graphs, depending on what variables you choose to investigate. Include information about mold types and their names in your project display.

Tips and Tricks

- The single greatest cause of poor results for this experiment is getting the bread too wet. Spray a light mist only.
- One factor that can affect mold growth is enclosure in the bag. Extend your project by modifying the "Go" procedure. Seal half your pieces in plastic bags and leave the other half out in the air. Or perhaps paper bags make a difference. How can you find out?

What's the Best Way to Stop Cut Fruits and Vegetables from Turning Brown?

TALK IT OVER:

What happens to slices of potato, apple, or banana if you leave them in air too long? Is there any way to keep them looking fresh longer?

GET:

- Cookie sheet
- Masking tape
- Pen
- 4 small bowls (or more)
- Water, lemon juice, vinegar, lemon-lime soda, or any other substance you would like to test
- Potato

- Knife
- Tweezers
- Camera (digital or with film)
- Access to a computer or photocopier (to make black-and-white pictures)
- Your grayscale (See "How to Make a Grayscale" in Part III)

GO

1. Stick a piece of masking tape to the cookie sheet. On the tape, write your labels, equal distances apart: none, water, lemon juice, vinegar, lemon-lime soda, and any others you have decided to test. Use masking tape to label your bowls in the same way.

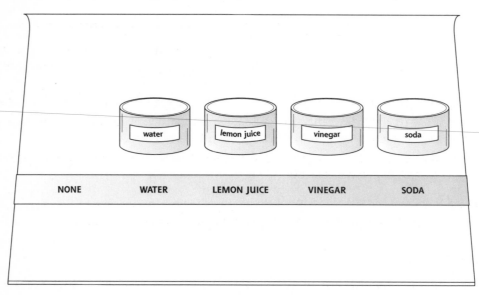

200

2. Pour each of the liquids you will test into its labeled bowl. The liquid needs to be about 2 cm (1 inch) deep.

3. Have an adult cut slices from the potato. Make the slices the same size, about 1 cm (less than ½ inch) thick.

4. Put 1 slice in each bowl. Make sure the liquid completely covers the slices. Let the slices stay in the bowls for about 1 minute. Keep 1 slice out; don't put it in any bowl.

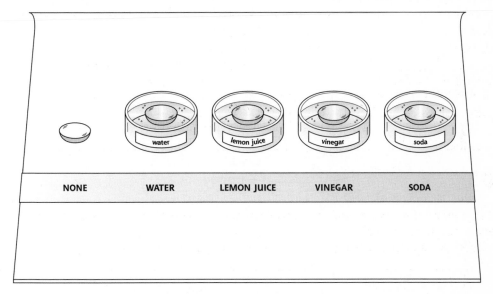

5. Using the tweezers, lift the slices from their bowls 1 at a time. Let the excess liquid drip from the slice into the bowl. Then place the slice on the cookie sheet, next to its label. Put the slice you kept out next to the "none" label.

6. Leave the slices for several hours. Check them often to see what changes you can observe.

7. When you see obvious differences, take a picture of the slices. Use your computer to print a black-and-white picture, or make a black-and-white copy on a photocopier.

8. Compare the colors of the slices to your grayscale. Assign each slice the number from the grayscale that best matches its color.

STAY SAFE:
Careful slicing those potatoes! Kitchen knives are sharp and can cut your fingers.

GO EASY

Test water and lemon juice against nothing (the air). Tell which slice turns darkest and which stays lightest. Try to explain why.

PLANTS

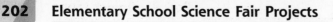

GO FAR

Commercial products that protect the color and flavor of cut fruits and vegetables contain ascorbic acid (vitamin C). Purchase such a product (Fruit-Fresh is an example) to compare with fruit juices and your own preparation made from crushed vitamin C pills.

Or you might find out whether Fruit-Fresh, citrus juices, or other preparations give better results with some foods than others. Use the "Go" procedure to test and compare slices of apple, banana, peach, pear, apricot, or avocado. Another idea is to dry two batches of peaches, one with Fruit-Fresh and one without. Conduct a blindfold test of taste preferences, using your friends and family as test subjects.

SHOW YOUR RESULTS:

Make a table like this for "Go Easy":

Liquid Tested	Circle the Result
None	Dark medium light
Water	Dark medium light
Lemon juice	Dark medium light

For "Go," show your slices and your pictures. Make a table of your results and a bar graph that compares the grayscale values. Suggest reasons that might explain the differences you observe.

Liquid Tested	Grayscale Value (1–10)
None (control)	
Water	
Lemon juice . . . and so on	

For "Go Far," makes tables and graphs to compare different test solutions and different fruits. If you conduct a taste test, make a table and a graph of people's preferences:

Batch	Number of People Who Preferred
Dried (no treatment)	
Dried with Fruit-Fresh	

Tips and Tricks

- Fruits and vegetables turn brown more quickly in a warm place. In a cool room, you may need to leave your experiment overnight. Your potato slices may turn darkest around the edges. You'll get better comparisons if you make your grayscale comparisons in the middle of the slice.

- To speed up the process, try whirling potato pieces in a food processor with a tablespoon of hydrogen peroxide. Can you explain why the potato browns so rapidly?

PLANTS

Are Some Fruits and Vegetables Denser than Others?

TALK IT OVER:

Why do some things float and other things sink? Ships that weigh tons float, so the difference can't depend on weight alone. The *volume* of the object, or how much space it takes up, makes a difference, too.

GET: _____

- Fruits and vegetables for testing (for example, potato, carrot, onion, kiwi, apple, orange, or others of your choice)
- Kitchen scale that weighs in grams
- Jar big enough to put the fruits and vegetables into

- Pan that the jar can sit in
- Pencil
- Measuring cup that measures volume in milliliters
- Calculator
- Towel

GO ➤

1. Weigh the food. Record the weight in grams.
2. Set the jar in the pan. Fill the jar with water to the brim, but don't let it run over.
3. Carefully put the food into the water. Record whether it floats or sinks.
4. If the food sinks, water will spill from the jar into the pan. If the food floats, push it down completely under the water with the point of the pencil so water spills out.

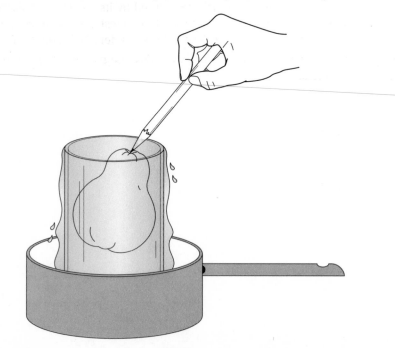

5. When water stops spilling over the top of the jar, remove the jar from the pan. Pour the water from the pan into the measuring cup. Measure and record the amount of water in milliliters. This equals the *volume* of the fruit or vegetable.

6. The density of the food is its weight in grams divided by its volume in milliliters. Use the calculator to find the density of each fruit and vegetable you test. For example, if the weight of an orange is 200 grams and its volume is 220 milliliters, its density is 200 g ÷ 220 ml = 0.9 g/ml.

7. Repeat steps 1–6 for each food you want to test. Dry the pan and the measuring cup with the towel between the tests.

STAY SAFE:
Wipe up spilled water from the floor immediately to prevent falls.

GO EASY

Put different fruits and vegetables in water. Observe and record whether they sink or float. Weigh the foods to show that some heavy ones float, while some lighter ones sink.

GO FAR

The density of pure water is 1 g/ml. (That's because 1 gram of water has a volume of 1 milliliter. 1 g ÷ 1 ml = 1 g/ml.) Use the procedure defined in "Go" to measure the density of objects around the house. Use your data to discover the mathematical rule that predicts whether objects sink or float. (**Hint:** How do the densities of objects that float and sink compare to the density of water?) Use the rule to explain why huge steel ships float, but tiny steel nails sink.

SHOW YOUR RESULTS:
Make a data table like this for "Go Easy":

Food Tested	Sink/Float (Tell Which)	Weight in grams

For "Go," arrange the foods in a data table from least to greatest density. Display samples of the foods you tested. Show some that sink in water and some that float. Display the tools you used to make your measurements.

Food Tested	Weight (in Grams)	Volume (in Milliliters)	Density# (Weight ÷ Volume)	Sink or Float (Tell Which)
Avocado				
Plum				
Pear . . . and so on				

Calculated value

For "Go Far," make a table like the "Go" table and display the objects that you measured for density. On a poster, show the mathematical rule that explains floating and sinking and tell why some very heavy objects can float while some very light ones sink. If you want to expand your project even further, try using density measurements to explain why an unpeeled orange floats, but a peeled orange sinks.

Tips and Tricks

Kitchen scales and measuring cups work fine for this project, but if you can borrow a metric balance and graduated cylinder from the school laboratory, you'll get better numbers.

Does a Mordant Make a Natural Dye Brighter or Longer Lasting?

TALK IT OVER:

Although most of the dyes (colors) in your clothes are human-made today, people centuries ago used plants to color their clothes. They also tested substances, called mordants, that they thought made the colors brighter or longer lasting. How can you test a mordant to see whether they were right?

GET:

- Water
- Measuring cup
- Small saucepan
- Set of measuring spoons
- Alum*
- Cream of tartar*

- Spoon for stirring
- 4 10-cm-x-10-cm (4"-x-4") squares of white, cotton fabric (perhaps cut from an old T-shirt)
- 2 safety pins
- Stove
- The outer skin from a yellow onion

GO

1. Into the small saucepan, measure 2 cups of water, 2 teaspoons of alum and ½ teaspoon of cream of tartar. Stir with the spoon to dissolve. This is the mordant you will test.

2. Pin a safety pin into each of 2 pieces of your cloth. Put these pieces in the saucepan. Set the other 2 pieces (without pins) aside.

3. Ask an adult to put the saucepan on the stove for you. Heat the water and the cloth to boiling. Reduce the heat and simmer for 10 minutes.

4. Ask the adult to discard the hot liquid for you. Let the fabric pieces dry overnight.

5. You now have four dry pieces of fabric. The two that have been treated with the mordant have pins in them.

6. Into a clean saucepan, measure 2 cups of water. Add the onion skins and all four pieces of fabric. Repeat steps 3 and 4.

7. When the pieces are dry, compare the colors. Did the mordant make a difference in the color?

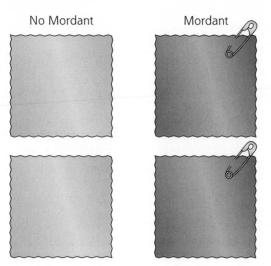

8. Set one mordant-treated piece and one untreated piece aside. Wash the other two pieces in a washing machine several times. Or leave them in a strong light for a few days. What happens to their color? How does it compare with the freshly dyed pieces?

STAY SAFE:

Do not attempt this experiment without adult help. The stove is hot, and boiling liquids can cause serious burns!

GO EASY

Skip testing the mordant. Simply experiment to see what colors you and your adult helper can get from different natural plant materials. Try dying white fabric with roots, bark, leaves, berries, twigs, fruit skins and pits, and more.

GO FAR

You can use the "Go" procedure to test a variety of other mordants, including vinegar and household ammonia. Your science teacher may be able to provide you with small amounts of potassium dichromate, iron (II) sulfate, tin (II) chloride, or copper (II) sulfate, which are also sometimes used as mordants. Try to design and carry out an experiment to test the question, How do different mordants interact with different natural dyes to affect how long color lasts after repeated washings (or after exposure to sunlight)?

SHOW YOUR RESULTS:

For "Go Easy," display your dyed fabric squares along with the plant materials you used to produce them.

For "Go," display your squares showing how the mordant affected the original color as well as the color after washing or exposure to sunlight. Write a paragraph that describes any differences and explains why you think they happened.

For "Go Far," make a table that shows the pieces you dyed and the mordants you tested. You might put them in a table like this:

Dye	Mordant			
	None	Alum and Cream of Tartar	Vinegar	Copper (II) Sulfate
Dandelion leaves	*Put fabric samples in these squares*			
Strawberries				
Grape skins . . . and so on				

Tips and Tricks

To compare the different mordants and treatments (washing or fading) most easily, put your fabric pieces side-by-side under a bright light and study the colors carefully. You *will* see differences that you can describe.

How Much Water Do Plants Lose to the Air?

TALK IT OVER:

Plants use water to make food and stay alive, but they are not 100 percent efficient. They lose some water to the air through tiny holes in their leaves. How can we find out how much water plants lose?

GET: _____

- 3 or more small potted plants, different kinds, in plastic pots
- Paper towels
- Kitchen scale or laboratory balance
- Water
- Clear plastic bags
- Plastic packing tape

GO

1. Water the plants until the soil is totally soaked and water runs out through the hole in the bottom of the pot.

2. Set the pots on a paper towel. Do not proceed until water stops running from the bottoms of the pots. Dry the outsides of the pots thoroughly.

3. Weigh the pots on the scale or balance. Record each weight.

4. Put a plastic bag over the top of each plant. Secure the bags to the pots with tape, like this:

5. Put the plant in a sunny spot for 1 hour or longer. Record the time and your observations.

6. Carefully remove the bags from the pots and weigh each pot again. Calculate water lost from the plant this way:

   weight after time in sun – original wet weight = water lost

7. Dry out the insides of the plastic bags with paper towels. Cover the plants again and reseal with tape. Return the plants to their sunny spot. Continue timing and weighing for several hours, perhaps several days, without adding any more water.

STAY SAFE:

Don't touch plant leaves if you have allergies. Wash your hands before and after handling the plants.

GO EASY

The "Go" procedure will work for you. Ask an adult to help you with the timing and weighing.

GO FAR

You'll get better results with this experiment if you conduct several trials and average your results. Also, collect data for several individual plants of each type. For example, you might test 3 philodendrons, 3 English ivies, and 3 spider plants.

Do some research to learn more about *transpiration*. If possible, borrow a microscope from your school's science lab and find the tiny holes in leaves, called *stomates*, that let water and gases pass in and out of the plant. Design and carry out your own investigation on stomate action. You might try using a light coating of petroleum jelly on the undersides of leaves to block stomates, then using the "Go" procedure to measure water loss.

SHOW YOUR RESULTS:

Put the amount of water lost in a data table like this for "Go" and "Go Easy":

Plant Tested	Amount of Water Lost*			
	9:20 a.m.	10:45 a.m.	11:30 a.m.	and so on
Philodendron				
Ivy				
Spider plant . . . and so on				

*Note that you are recording the *calculated* value for water lost, but don't lose your actual weights. Keep them in your notes and report them with the results of your investigation.

For "Go Far," modify the table to include each of the plants you test. Add a row for averages.

For all the experiments, make bar or line graphs that show the water lost from your plants (on the vertical axis) as time goes on (the horizontal axis). Write a few sentences comparing water loss in your plants and draw some conclusions about which of your plants lost the most. Display your plants with your project. For "Go Far," you might also display a microscope and some slides of stomates.

Tips and Tricks

- Don't use terra cotta pots. They are porous and lose water through their surfaces. If you use plants in plastic pots, your only losses will be from the soil surface (which you can safely assume is the same for all the plants) and from the leaves.
- Small plants are easier to handle than large plants in this experiment. You'll find tiny houseplants in the gardening section of most discount stores and home improvement centers.

PLANTS

Do Long Pods Contain More Green Beans?

TALK IT OVER:

Where are the beans in a green bean? Are all green beans alike? Do longer pods have more beans than shorter pods do? How can you find out?

GET: _____

- 30 fresh whole green beans
- Metric ruler
- Calculator

GO

1. The project isn't hard, but it requires patience and careful counting. Get 30 fresh green beans. Make a data table like this:

Bean	Length	Number of Beans
1		
2		
3 and so on . . .		
Average		

2. Pick up the first bean. Measure its length with your ruler. If it's curved, straighten it out along your ruler so you get an accurate measure of its length. Record the length of the pod in millimeters.

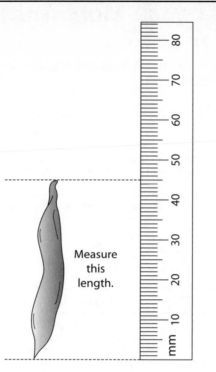

3. Open the bean pod and count the number of beans inside. Record that number.

4. Repeat steps 2 and 3 for each bean until you have data for 30 beans.

5. Calculate the average pod length and the average number of beans per pod. Record the averages in the data table.

STAY SAFE:

Don't eat the beans after you have handled them. Put them in your garden compost pile if you have one.

GO EASY

Investigate a simpler question. Ask the following question: How does the number of beans in a green bean pod vary? To answer it, do not measure the length of the pods. Instead, find the *frequency* of each bean count. (Frequency is how often a number appears in a set of data.) To do that, first count the number of beans inside each pod. Then count how many pods had each number of beans inside. Record the totals in a table like this:

Number of Beans (in a Pod)	Number of Pods (That Had This Number of Beans)
0	
1	
2	
3	
4	
5	
6 and so on	
Total	30

Then make a *frequency* graph. Put the number of beans in a pod along the horizontal axis. Put the number of pods on the vertical axis. Then make a bar of the correct height for each. Your graph will tell you how much your pods vary. If you have a wide, low graph, your beans vary a lot. If your graph is tall and narrow, your beans do not vary much.

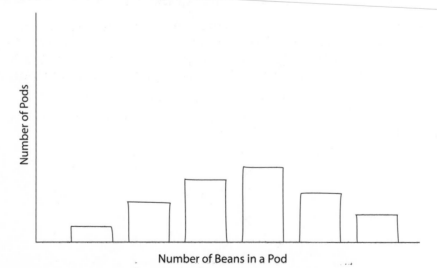

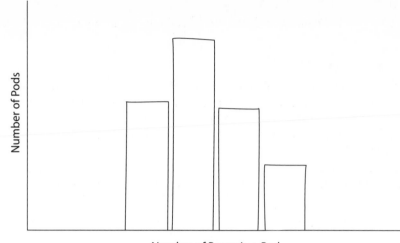

Number of Beans in a Pod

GO FAR

Get data for 100 beans. (Yes, that's a lot of beans, but you want a good project, don't you?)

After you make your scatterplot (see the next page), calculate a *correlation coefficient* (often called *r*). It's a number that indicates how two variables relate. The formula for finding *r* is a little complicated, and it is most easily done with a calculator or software program. Ask your math teacher for help or go online to learn more.

SHOW YOUR RESULTS:

The "Go" and "Go Far" projects ask you to look for a *correlation* between pod length and number of beans in a pod. (*Correlate* means vary together in some predictable way.) If longer pods have more beans, then the correlation is positive. If they have fewer, then the correlation is negative. If pod length does not predict the number of beans, then there is no correlation.

The first step toward finding a correlation is a scatterplot graph. Use your data table to make the graph. Put pod length along the horizontal axis. Put number of beans along the vertical axis. Then, for your first bean, find the point where its pod length and its number of beans intersect. Put a dot at that point. For example, if your first bean was 55 millimeters long and had 6 beans inside, your first dot would be placed like this:

PLANTS

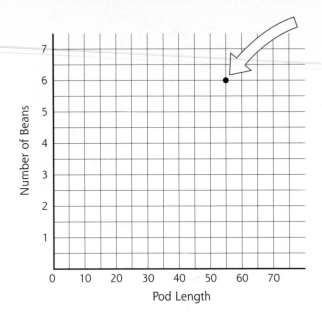

After you have made a dot for every bean, look at where the dots are. If they appear to lie (more or less) along a straight line, then draw it. If your line slants upward, you *may* have a positive correlation. If it slants down, you *may* have a negative correlation. If the points are so spread out that no line seems to match them, you *may* have found that pod length and number of beans are not correlated.

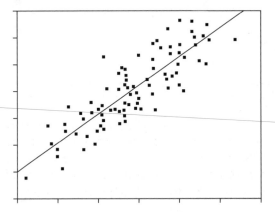

Possible Positive Correlation

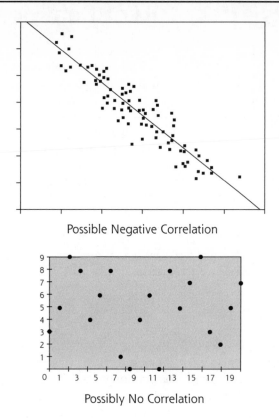

Possible Negative Correlation

Possibly No Correlation

Tips and Tricks

- Scatterplots can be deceiving. Sometimes they appear to show a correlation that isn't really there. Or they can fail to reveal a correlation that really exists. Get a teacher, parent, or math expert friend to help you interpret your scatterplots.

- Take your project further by comparing fresh beans to the canned and frozen kinds.

- Try using this method to compare the seed counts of different varieties of peas, oranges, apples, or grapefruit.

How Do Odors Affect Cricket Behavior?

TALK IT OVER:

Is the sense of smell important to survival in animals? How do some animals familiar to you respond to certain smells? How can you test the response of crickets to odors?

GET:

- Shoebox
- Live crickets,* 12 or more
- Cotton balls
- Extracts purchased from the spice aisle at the supermarket (try vanilla, almond, peppermint, and others)

- Other subtances to test, such as perfumes, household cleaners, skin care products, spices, or essential oils (from the health foods store) and others

Note: You can maintain crickets for weeks in any small, ventilated box equipped with pieces of egg carton for shelter and a slice of apple for food and moisture.

GO

1. Put the crickets in the box. (It is okay to shake them gently from their egg carton homes. You will not hurt them.)

2. Watch them for at least 5 minutes. Make careful notes of everything you see them doing. These observations will serve as your control.

3. Put a few drops of an extract on a cotton ball. Put the cotton ball in the box with the crickets. Watch again for 5 minutes or more, carefully recording anything the crickets do in response to the extract.

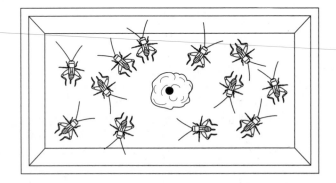

4. Remove the cotton ball and discard it. Give your crickets 10 minutes to rest. Then use a fresh cotton ball and test another substance, just as you did in step 3. Record all your observations carefully.

STAY SAFE:

The crickets will not hurt you, but be sure to wash your hands before and after this experiment.

GO EASY

The "Go" procedure will work for you.

GO FAR

Use the "Go" procedure to design and carry out an investigation to determine which type of insect repellent should be most effective at keeping "bugs" away (assuming mosquitoes act anything like crickets).

SHOW YOUR RESULTS:

Record your observations in a table like this:

Odor Tested	What I Observed The Crickets Doing
None (control)	
Vanilla	
Peppermint . . . and so on	

Write summaries of all your observation and make comparative statements such as, "Extract X attracted the crickets. I concluded this because 7 of my 12 crickets moved closer to it and they moved their antennae around more than the controls did. Extract Z repelled them. Ten of my 12 crickets ran away from the odor, and they ran fast!"

Tips and Tricks

- If you don't shake your shoebox around very much, you needn't worry about your crickets hopping out. They'll stay in the box. If they are getting away from you, use a taller box for your observations.
- The warmer the room, the more your crickets will move around. To make your observations easier, work in a cool place.
- Be patient and look closely. Crickets do many interesting things. Try to describe them in as much detail as you can.

BEHAVIOR

How Do Crickets Respond to Light and Dark?

TALK IT OVER:

What do you see dogs, cats, birds, insects, and other animals doing? How do they respond to changes in their environment? What do you think crickets might do if they have a choice between light and dark places?

GET:

- Opaque plastic shoebox with a transparent lid
- Ruler
- Marker
- Live crickets,* 12 or more

- Stopwatch or kitchen timer with seconds
- Desk lamp
- Dark-colored towel

Note: You can maintain crickets for weeks in any small, ventilated box equipped with pieces of egg carton for shelter and a slice of apple for food and moisture.

GO

1. Measure the length of the box lid. Find the midpoint. Use the marker to draw a line on the lid across the middle, like this:

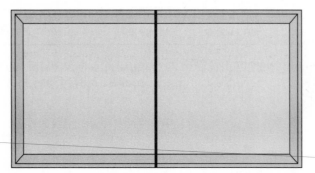

2. Put the open box under the desk lamp. Turn the lamp on.
3. Put the crickets into the box. (It is okay to shake them gently from their egg carton homes. You will not hurt them.)

4. Put the lid on the box. Put the lamp close to the top of the box. Make sure the box is evenly lighted—no dark corners!

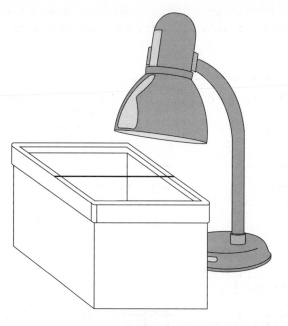

5. Watch the crickets for about 10 minutes. Make notes about things you see them doing.
6. Gently, without jiggling the crickets too much, place the towel over ½ of the lid.
7. Start the stopwatch. Every 15 seconds, record the number of crickets you count in the light side of the box. Keep counting and recording for 3 minutes or longer.

STAY SAFE:
Be careful with the desk lamp. The bulb can get very hot and burn your fingers.

GO EASY

Follow the "Go" procedure, but count and record numbers ever 30 seconds instead of every 15.

GO FAR

Follow the "Go" procedure, repeating the experiment three or more times and averaging your results. From your average data, calculate the *percent* of the crickets that remain in the light, using this formula:

(number of crickets in the light ÷ total number of crickets) × 100 = percent in the light

Note that the percent of the crickets in the dark equals 100 percent minus the percent in the light. Or

percent in the light + percent in the dark = 100 percent

BEHAVIOR

You may also design and conduct experiments to see how crickets respond to differences in temperature, moisture, or some other condition in the environment. Or you might try similar experiments with other readily available animals such as mealworms or maggots (available from bait shops).

SHOW YOUR RESULTS:

Record numbers in a data table like this for "Go Easy":

Time	Number in Light	Number in Dark	Total
0 seconds			12
30 seconds			12
1 minute			12
1 minute 30 seconds			12
2 minutes			12
2 minutes 30 seconds			12
3 minutes			12

Make a bar graph to show differences.

Use the same kind of data table and bar graph for "Go," but record data every 15 seconds.

For "Go Far," include percents in your data tables. Make a master table that averages your results from three trials. Make a line graph of average percents by time. Use different color lines to show percents of crickets in light and dark conditions. State a possible explanation for any differences you measured. Make similar tables and graphs for any other experiments you conduct.

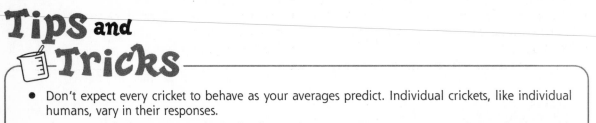

Tips and Tricks

- Don't expect every cricket to behave as your averages predict. Individual crickets, like individual humans, vary in their responses.
- If you can't find an opaque plastic shoebox with a transparent top, use an ordinary shoebox with a sheet of glass or clear plastic on top.

Does the Caffeine in Soft Drinks Affect the Human Heart Rate?

TALK IT OVER:

According to the National Soft Drink Association, most 12-ounce cans of soda contain approximately 45 milligrams of caffeine. By comparison, a 7-ounce cup of coffee contains approximately 100 milligrams of caffeine. Caffeine is also found in tea, chocolate, and some over-the-counter medicines (check the labels). What is caffeine? What effect might it have on how fast the heart beats?

Note: Before you begin, learn how to take a person's pulse. You'll find directions for taking the pulse (counting heartbeats) in many health books and Web sites. Practice recording the pulse rate for 1 minute exactly (using a stopwatch) until you are sure you can do it accurately every time.

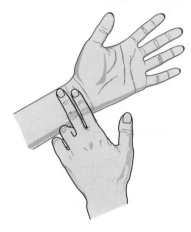

GET:

- 10 or more adults who are willing to help you
- Personal music player with earphones and soothing music (such as *Pachelbel Canon*)
- Eye mask
- Comfortable chair
- 10 or more cans of a soft drink that contains caffeine
- Clock and stopwatch

GO

1. Arrange a time for testing each adult. Each test will require about 30 minutes of the adult's time. Ideally, you should test each of your subjects at the same time of day, in the same place, using the same music, and so on—that is, keep all your test conditions as much the same as possible.

2. Ask each of your subjects to eat or drink nothing for at least 2 hours before the test.

3. Test your subjects one at a time. Seat the person in a comfortable chair. Put a mask over the person's eyes. Ask the person to listen to soothing music and relax completely for 5 minutes. Then, disturbing the person as little as possible, take his or her pulse for 1 minute. Record.

4. Then ask the adult to drink the can of soft drink as quickly as possible, while still relaxing in the chair. After the subject finishes the drink, wait exactly 5 minutes, then measure and record the pulse rate for 1 minute.

5. Take the 1-minute pulse rate again every 5 minutes until you have at least 4 readings.

STAY SAFE:
No special precautions for this project!

GO EASY

Get an adult helper to take pulse rates for you. Take pulse rates only twice: once before drinking the soda and again 15 minutes later.

GO FAR

Test different brands of soft drinks. (Visit the manufacturers' Web sites to determine how much caffeine the drinks contain.) You might also try testing different kinds of chocolate or varieties of sports or energy drinks. Or, try testing people who regularly drink sodas or coffee in comparison with people who don't. Do their responses differ?

If you have more time and your subjects are willing to be tested several times, have an adult make instant coffee drinks that vary in caffeine content. For example, you might dissolve ½ teaspoon of instant coffee in ½ cup of water for the first test. You might double or triple that amount for subsequent tests. Use the "Go" procedure to see whether greater amounts of caffeine produce different results than lesser amounts.

SHOW YOUR RESULTS:

Put pulse rates in a data table like this for "Go":

Subject	Relaxed Pulse Rate	Pulse rate after soda				
		5 Minutes	10 Minutes	15 Minutes	20 Minutes	Change (20 Minutes – Relaxed Rate)
Mom						
Dad						
Uncle Eddie . . . and so on						
Average (total of all pulse rates ÷ number of subjects)						

Make a line graph of the average pulse rates over time. Make line graphs that show the differences among individuals. (You may find big changes in some people and smaller or no changes in others.)

For "Go Easy," use a data table like this:

Subject	Relaxed Pulse Rate	Pulse Rate After 15 Minutes
Mom		
Dad		
Uncle Eddie . . . and so on		

Make a bar graph for each person you test. Use two bars on each graph to show how each person's after-drink pulse rate compares with the before-drink rate.

For "Go Far," use data tables and line graphs as for "Go," comparing the drinks or amounts of caffeine you test.

Tips and Tricks

Be careful about the conclusions you draw. The drink you tested contains caffeine, but it also contains other ingredients such as sugar or artificial sweetener. Therefore, caffeine *may* be responsible for any differences you observed, but you cannot be sure, because you did not test pure caffeine.

How Accurate and Precise Are Dart Players?

TALK IT OVER:

Are some family members or friends better at darts than you are? What makes a good dart player? How can we measure the difference among people's performance at darts?

GET:

- Dart board
- 3 darts
- Camera

- Ruler
- 3 or more willing dart players

GO

1. Ask a dart player to throw 3 darts into the board. The goal is to hit the bull's-eye in the center. Let a player who misses the board try again until 3 darts are stuck in the board.

2. Take a picture of this player's darts.

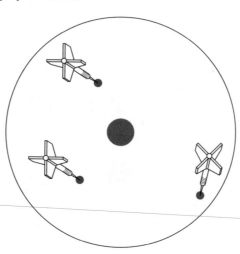

3. With the ruler, measure
   - The distance between the darts (comparing two at a time)

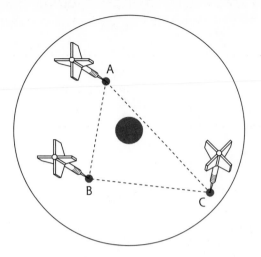

   - The distance of each dart from the center of the bull's-eye.

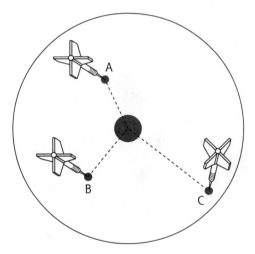

4. Repeat steps 1–3 with each dart player you test.

In everyday talk, we use the words *precise* and *accurate* as if they mean the same thing. They don't—at least not in the science of measurement. Precision is how uniform or consistent measurements are. For the dart player, it is how close together the darts are. In this experiment, the average distance between darts is a measure of precision. Accuracy is different. It is the quality of the result, or how close it comes to the true value. In this case, the true value is the goal of the game, hitting the bull's-eye. The average distance to the bull's-eye is a measurement of accuracy.

The following result is precise, but not very accurate:

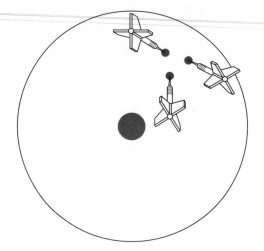

The following result is accurate, but not very precise:

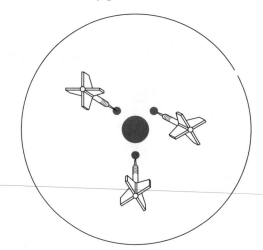

The following result is both precise and accurate:

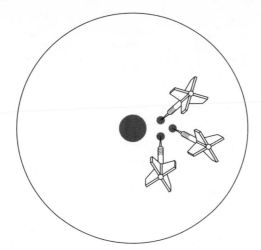

So, to analyze your data, calculate for each player

- **Precision:** the average distance between the darts:

$$\frac{(\text{distance A to B}) + (\text{distance B to C}) + (\text{distance C to A})}{3} = \text{average distance}$$

- **Accuracy:** the average distance between the bull's-eye and the darts:

$$\frac{(\text{distance bull to A}) + (\text{distance bull to B}) + (\text{distance bull to C})}{3} = \text{average distance to bull}$$

STAY SAFE:

Stay out of the way when darts are being thrown, and do not horse around with darts. Even plastic-tipped ones can cause injury.

GO EASY

Get an adult to help you with setups, measurements, photography, and calculations.

GO FAR

Expand your project by giving your dart players practice time. Limit them to 10 practice throws or 5 minutes of practice—whatever you like, as long as each player gets the same treatment. Then measure and calculate distances as you did in "Go." Compare it to each player's pre-practice performance. Try to answer the following question: How does practice affect the precision and accuracy of dart players?

SHOW YOUR RESULTS:

Record your measurements and calculations in data tables like these:

Precision: Distance Between Darts				
Player	**A to B**	**B to C**	**C to A**	**Average**
Jessica				
Brad				
Jamal . . . and so on				

Accuracy: Distance to Bull's-Eye				
Player	**Dart A**	**Dart B**	**Dart C**	**Average**
Jessica				
Brad				
Jamal . . . and so on				

For "Go Easy" and "Go," make bar graphs that compare the average precision and the average accuracy of the players. Display your pictures to show how accuracy and precision varied.

For "Go Far," make bar graphs that show the change in accuracy and precision after practice. The average difference pre- and post-practice will tell you whether practice improved performance. Your graphs will show how individuals varied in the effect of practice.

Tips and Tricks

- Measure in millimeters from tip to tip for the distance between darts.
- Measure in millimeters from the exact center of the bull's-eye to the dart tip.

How Reliable are Eyewitness Reports?

TALK IT OVER:

Is seeing believing? How certain are you of your facts when you see something happen? How sure can you be that people are reporting correctly when they tell you what they saw or heard?

GET: _____

- Access to a television that records or a DVD player
- 5 or more volunteer test subjects
- Tape recorder

GO

1. Record a short scene (10 minutes or less) from a television show. Select a scene that has many characters and lots of action. Or you might use a short segment from a DVD. Try to select a scene that will not be familiar to your subjects.

2. Write a quiz about the scene. Ask specific questions such as the precise words a particular character used or who was in the scene when something important happened. Also, ask for details such as the color of someone's hair or whether a certain character was taller or older than another.

3. One at a time, have each of your volunteer subjects view the scene. When it is over, turn on your tape recorder and interview each of your witnesses. Ask your list of questions and record the answers on tape. Do not interrupt, correct, or assist your interviewees in any way.

4. Later, when you are on your own, listen to the taped answers. Make data tables summarizing the responses from all your subjects. Analyze your data in several ways. You might determine, for example,

   a. The average number of right answers

   b. Which questions evoked the greatest number of wrong answers

   c. The percent accuracy for each question:

   (the number of people who got it right ÷
   the total number of people who answered the question) × 100

   d. Which questions produced the widest diversity in your subjects' responses

STAY SAFE:

Whenever you use human subjects in an experiment, be sure to behave in a courteous manner and treat your subjects with respect. Don't use a violent or obscene recording for this experiment. Don't ask your subjects personal questions. Don't insult or embarrass your subjects in any way.

GO EASY

Get an adult's help with the planning, recording, interviewing, and data analysis.

GO FAR

You can expand your project by adding other measures of human perception and memory. Try asking your subjects the same questions again 2, 3, or 5 days after they view the recording. Or test two groups of subjects: interview people in one group immediately after the viewing, but wait 24 hours to interview people in the other group. Try asking some trick questions that lead your subjects to say what you want them to. How effective is such questioning in shaping what people think they saw?

SHOW YOUR RESULTS:

Your data tables will depend on how you designed and carried out your experiment. Start with a simple table like this:

Question	How Many Subjects Got It Right?	Percent Accuracy

Write short paragraphs stating your conclusions about how reliable your eyewitnesses were and which details produced the greatest number of witness errors. If possible, show your TV recording as part of your project display. Provide copies of your quiz so viewers of your project can test their observational skills for themselves.

Tips and Tricks

- The more test subjects you interview, the more reliable your data will be.
- The success of this project will depend in large part on the questions you ask. State them clearly and make them specific enough to distinguish the eagle-eyed observers from their less attentive peers.
- Make sure the test conditions are the same for all your subjects. Test them in a quiet room away from distractions. If possible, test them all at the same time of day. Don't allow interruptions during the testing, and don't chat with your subjects before, during, or immediately after the test session.

Part 3
Additional Information

How to Make a Grayscale

Several of the project ideas in Part II suggest that you make and use a grayscale. A *grayscale* allows you to assign a number value to a difference in color that might otherwise be described only in vague, comparative terms, such as lighter or darker. A grayscale provides objective, numerical rankings, because color and value are not the same thing.

- A color may be red, green, blue, or any of the others that we recognize.
- Value, in contrast, is how light or dark a color is. In paints and tints, it's how much black is added. Colors that have little, if any, black are light colors. Darker colors have more black.

The human eye can be fooled, and our brains can easily confuse color and value; making and using a grayscale ends the confusion. It allows students to compare a black-and-white picture of whatever they are working on against a known standard. The standard assigns a 1 to 10 ranking to black, white, and shades of gray. In the sample grayscale in this chapter, I use 1 to represent a nearly pure white. 10 represents a nearly pure black. The grays in-between get darker from 1 to 10.

You may find a grayscale published in a book or on a Web site. If you don't, you can easily make your own.

Get:

- Sheet of translucent plastic*
- Ruler
- Ballpoint pen
- Stapler
- Scissors
- Access to a photocopy machine
- Black felt or foam*
- Labels

Procedure:

1. Cut the plastic into 10 strips, each about 1 inch (2.5 cm) wide.
2. Place the strips in a pile, all 10 on top of one another. Slide them into a staggered arrangement, so that you expose squares approximately 1 inch in size. The bottom square is one layer of plastic thick. The next square is 2 layers, and so on, until the area at the top of the pile is 10 layers thick.

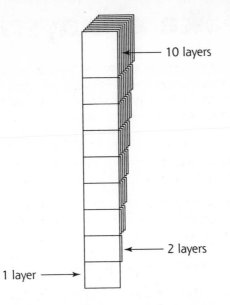

3. Staple the strips together at the top and trim away the excess.

4. Take the strips to a black-and-white photocopy machine and turn the pile cut side down. Put a piece of black foam or felt on top of the pile. Make a copy. If necessary, adjust the light-dark setting on the machine until you achieve a good range of values from black to white.

5. Put labels beside the squares. Label your grayscale from 1 for white to 10 for black.

To use your grayscale, place it beside a black-and-white photograph or photocopy of the experimental results you want to evaluate. Then assign from the grayscale the numbers that most closely match what you see in your data. From these numbers, you can make comparisons. If, for example, you studied browning in fruit, you might observe that Treatment 1 for the fruit resulted in a gray value of 3, while Treatment 2 produced a 5. If the desired objective is to prevent the fruit from discoloring, you might conclude that Treatment 1 is the more effective treatment.

Sources of Materials

In some of the "Get" lists throughout this book, you may have noticed an asterisk (*) after an item. Items marked in this way may not be readily available in your area or may take a little (but not too much) searching to find. This chapter describes those materials and tells where you can find them locally or order them by mail or online. In some cases, I note the manufacturer of the product we used, but you may find others that work just as well. Full contact information on scientific supply houses is included in the following chapter, "Science Suppliers." You may want to request a catalog from one or more of them. These companies are good sources of materials, and their catalogs are a wealth of ideas and opportunities for the serious science student.

Material	Manufacturer	Availability
Alum		Available in the spice aisle of most supermarkets. It is used for making pickles. If not available there, ask a drugstore to order it for you.
Bamboo		Available at hardware stores, garden shops, and home improvement stores. I got mine at Home Depot.
Bar magnets (small)	RoseArt Magnetix Magnetic Building Set (Do not purchase the Magnetix X-treme set, which contains triangular magnets.)	Toy stores and toy departments. I got mine at Wal-Mart. Bar magnets in a variety of sizes are available from science supply companies.
Brine shrimp (*Artemia*) eggs		Aquarium stores and pet shops sell *Artemia* eggs. They show up in toy stores as "Sea Monkey" growing kits. I ordered mine from Carolina Biological Supply.
Button magnets (¾ inch)		Craft shops and office supply stores
Cellophane: clear, red, blue, and green		The gift wrap section of drugstores, department stores, and discount houses

Material	Manufacturer	Availability
Compass with a number scale	The Instructional Compass by Suunto, Model A-1000	Check camping and sporting goods stores. I ordered mine from The Compass Store, a division of ROC Gear 4045 Inman Park Lane Buford, GA 30519 770-614-1233 www.thecompassstore.com
Crickets, live		Purchase from aquarium supply shops, bait shops, or pet stores (in the fish food department). Or you can order a kit for raising your own from Carolina Biological.
Dropper that measures in milliliters		Look for the milliliter scale printed on the side of the large plastic dropper. Available from drugstores and discount houses.
Electrical tester (measures voltage, current, resistance)	Made by many companies. I used one from Commercial Electric.	These projects test low voltages and small amounts of current, so get one that has a 0–250mA DC current range and 0–10 DC voltage range. Choose one that has settings for testing batteries and reading their outputs in the 1.5 to 9V range. Such testers are widely available in hardware, building supply, and home improvement stores. I got mine at Home Depot.
Foam, black, peel-and-stick	I used a sheet of black, 2 mm thick Foamies manufactured by Darice, Inc. (www.darice.com)	Available at craft stores and in scrapbooking supply departments.
Fresnel lens (magnifying sheet)		Sold for help in reading telephone book and instruction sheets. Also sold in camper and automotive supply shops to use as magnifiers on the back windows of RVs. I ordered mine from The Science eStore at www.physlink.com/estore

(continued)

Material	Manufacturer	Availability
Iodine solution	Equivalent to a 1 percent iodine solution sold for first aid use. One brand name is Betadine.	Drugstores
Metal rods, 12" x $^1/_{16}$" diameter: copper, steel, and brass or other metals	K & S Engineering (www.ksmetals.com)	Available in hardware stores and hobby shops. I got mine at Hobby Lobby.
Minerals		Get them at a local rock shop or order them from a science supply house, such as Carolina or Ward's.
Mirrors, plastic, 4" x 5"		Available in plastic supply stores, craft shops, and some framing shops. I ordered mine from Learning Things, Inc. at www.learningthings.us/index.html
Plastic, translucent, not colored (for making a grayscale)	I cut mine from a set of Table of Contents Ready Index Presentation Dividers manufactured by Avery Dennison Office Products	Office supply stores
Plastic, translucent colored	I cut mine from the backs of Staples report covers	Other brands available in office supply stores will work. Just make sure you get blue, red, and yellow in a variety that lets some light pass through.
Solar cell	Solar World (www.solar-world.com)	I ordered mine from Science Kit. Also available from Radio Shack.
Sound-activated finder		Several brands and models are available and they operate in slightly different ways. They are often available in electronics stores, hardware stores, and online. I ordered mine from www.overstock.com
Sound-activated switch kit	Model K-36 from Elenco Electronics, Inc. (www.elenco.com)	I ordered mine from The Science eStore at www.physlink.com/estore

Material	Manufacturer	Availability
Sound frequency computer software		A number of programs are available. Some of them are freeware or shareware that can be downloaded from the Internet. The programs split sounds into their basic frequencies and display them on a graph. One good one is Canary, a package developed by Bioacoustics Research program at Cornell University. Learn more about it at http://birds.cornell.edu/brp/CanaryInfo.html
Sound-level meter		Sound-level meters are available in many different makes and models, costing anywhere from about $30 to $2,000 or more. For this project, it may be best to borrow a meter from a school or college physics lab. Or you may find an affordable model at your local Radio Shack or online at outlets such as www.amazon.com
Sunprint paper	Manufactured by Lawrence Hall of Science	Science museum shops and homeschooling catalogs. I ordered mine from Science Kit.
Test strips for pH and total alkalinity	AquaChek Pool and Spa Test Strips from Environmental Test Systems Hach Company (www.aquachek.com)	Spa and pool suppliers or service companies.
Thermometer, digital, instant-read	Acu-Rite (imported by Chaney Instrument Company)	Kitchen supply shops and departments. I got mine in the kitchenware section at Wal-Mart.
Thermometer, indoor-outdoor tube type		Available at hardware stores, garden shops, discount houses, and home improvement stores. I got mine at Wal-Mart.
UV Intensity Meter and Lens Tester card	Measurement and Technology Company	I ordered mine from Science Kit. May be available at your local Radio Shack.

Science Suppliers

The following companies are good sources of hard-to-find and specialized materials. Their catalogs and Web sites may also give you some good ideas for projects.

AccuLab Products Group
614 Scenic Drive, Suite #104
Modesto, CA 95350
209-522-8874
www.sensornet.com

Arbor Scientific
P.O. Box 2750
Ann Arbor, MI 48106
800-367-6695
www.arborsci.com

Blue Spruce Scientific Supply
5455 Spine Road, Suite C
Boulder, CO 80301
800-825-8522
http://bluebio.com

Carolina Biological Supply Company
2700 York Rd.
Burlington, NC 27215
800-334-5551
www.carolina.com

Connecticut Valley Biological
82 Valley Road
P.O. Box 326
Southampton, MA 01073
800-628-7748
www.ctvalleybio.com

Delta Education
80 Northwest Blvd.
P.O. Box 3000
Nashua, NH 03061-3000
800-258-1302
www.delta-education.com

Edmund Scientific Co.
60 Pearce Ave.
Tonawanda, NY 14150
800-728-6999
http://scientificsonline.com

Fisher Science Education
4500 Turnberry Drive
Hanover Park, IL 60133
800-955-1177
https://www1.fishersci.com/education/index.jsp

Frey Scientific
P.O. Box 8101
100 Paragon Parkway
Mansfield, OH 44903
800-225-3739
www.freyscientific.com

LaMotte Company
P.O. Box 329
802 Washington Ave.
Chestertown, MD 21620
800-344-3100
www.lamotte.com

Learning Things, Inc.
4381 34th Street South
St. Petersburg, FL 33711
727-864-6567
www.learningthings.us/index.html

NASCO–Fort Atkinson
901 Janesville Avenue
P.O. Box 901
Fort Atkinson, WI 53538-0901
800-558-9595
www.enasco.com

PASCO Scientific
10101 Foothills Blvd.
Roseville, CA 95747
800-772-8700
www.pasco.com

Schoolmasters Science
745 State Circle, Box 1941
Ann Arbor, MI 48106
800-521-2832
www.schoolmasters.com

Science eStore
5318 E. 2nd Street #530
Long Beach, CA 90803
888-438-9867
www.physlink.com/estore

Science Kit
777 E. Park Drive
PO Box 5003
Tonawanda, NY 14150
800-828-7777
www.sciencekit.com

Ward's Natural Science
PO Box 92912
Rochester, NY 14692-9012
800-962-2660
www.wardsci.com

Making Graphs

If a picture is worth a thousand words, a graph is worth ten thousand numbers. Trends and relationships can hide in data tables, but they pop out from graphs. No science project is complete without one.

Making a graph is not difficult, and computer software can help. A computer banishes plotting errors, but it can't decide what kind of graph is right for your data or on what axes the variables belong. Those decisions belong to the student experimenter.

If you have completed an experimental project, you have worked with two very important variables:

- The independent variable, which you changed in some systematic way on purpose
- The dependent variable, which you measured as your outcome variable

Your dependent variable reveals whether the independent variable had some effect on the results.

When making a graph, put the independent variable on the horizontal, or *x*-axis. Put the dependent variable on the vertical, or *y*-axis. Why? Because that's the way it has always been done, and we have learned to read them that way, whether we realize it or not. This is convention, but it's a convention that demands respect. A graph set up on the wrong axes is more confusing than enlightening.

Put the independent variable here.

Deciding whether to make a bar graph or a line graph requires a look at the independent variable:

- Use a bar graph for a *discontinuous independent variable*. This is a discrete variable that does not change in some consistent or mathematical way. If your independent variable is words, not numbers, you probably have a discontinuous variable and you want to use a bar graph. Examples of discontinuous variables are colors, brands of a product, names of metals, makes of batteries, and so on. **Note:** Some computer software packages call bar graphs of the type described here *column graphs*. If you are using a software package of this type, select column graph as your graph type.

- Use a line graph for a *continuous independent variable*. This is a consistent, mathematical variable. If your independent variable is numbers, you probably have a continuous variable and you want to use a line graph. Examples of continuous variables are time, distance, wavelengths of light, height, percentages, speed, or degrees of direction.

Once the axes are established and the correct kind of graph selected, the rest is mechanical. You can use computer software if you want, but it is not hard to make graphs on graph paper. The scale along the axis for any continuous variable is simply a number line. Choose a convenient unit of measure, such as 1 square on the graph paper, and allow it to represent a unit of measure in your experiment. Choose a unit that will let you get all your numbers, from 0 to your largest measurement, on the axis. The units will not be the same on the two axes. For example, time plotted on the horizontal axis might be 1 square = 1 minute. Temperature on the vertical axis might be 1 square = 5°C. For bar graphs, the vertical axis is a number line. The horizontal has word labels for each discontinuous variable, placed at equal distances to make bars of equal width.

Once the scales are established and the number lines labeled, the next step is to find the points where the variable values intersect. Once all the points are plotted, you may connect the dots to make a line graph—or, in some cases, draw a smooth line that estimates their best-fit trend. For bar graphs, draw bars to the height of the plotted point. Check the graph to make sure both axes are labeled. Give the graph a title. If it has more than one line or more than one dependent variable is plotted, add a legend with the appropriate color code.

Note important features of graphs in the following examples:

Example 1: Erica used a water test kit to measure the level of nitrate in a pond near her home. She measured nitrate in water samples that she collected before, during, and after a rainstorm. She put her dependent variable, nitrate concentration, on the vertical axis. She put her independent variable, the time in relation to rain, on the horizontal. Because it was a discontinuous variable, she made a bar graph.

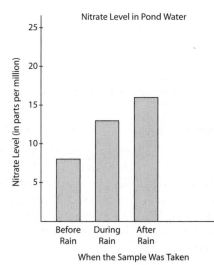

Example 2: Nigel investigated whether water temperature affects the respiratory rate of goldfish. He counted the number of gill beats per minute at 6 different temperatures. He put his dependent variable, gill beats per minute, on the vertical axis. He put his independent variable, temperature, on the horizontal axis. Because his independent variable was continuous, he made a line graph.

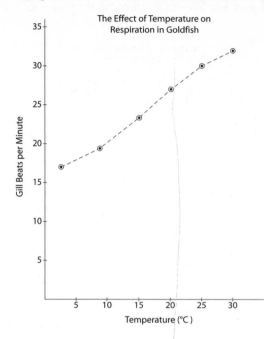

Example 3: Juanita studied bean plants she grew in light and dark conditions. She measured and calculated the average height of 10 plants grown in each condition every day for 9 days. Juanita realized that she could get both her independent variables—light/dark and day of measurement—on a single line graph. She put the days on her horizontal axis. She put her plant's average heights on the vertical. She used a legend and different kinds of lines to compare plants grown under the light and dark conditions.

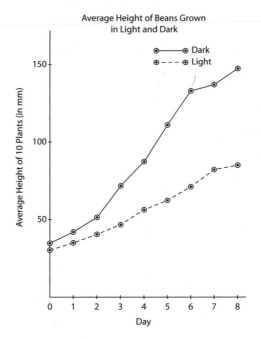

Bar and line graphs are easy to make and interpret, and they prove valuable in many situations. They are, however, only two among many graphing options available to student experimenters. The type of data collected determines whether other graphing forms are appropriate. The best source of advice in such cases is a math teacher.

Using the Metric System

If you want to work as scientists do, use the metric system. It's a simple, convenient, easy-to-use system based on multiples of ten. But if you yearn for the familiarity of inches, pounds, and pints, you can easily convert. This chapter reviews some of the most common and useful metric units and their U.S. equivalents.

Length

The standard unit of length in the metric system is the meter. One meter contains 100 centimeters and 1,000 millimeters.

1 millimeter = 0.001 meter

1 meter = 1,000 millimeters

1 centimeter = 0.01 meter

1 meter = 100 centimeters

Abbreviate these lengths as follows:

1 millimeter = 1 mm

1 centimeter = 1 cm

1 meter = 1 m

Comparisons to the U.S. system: A meter is about 39 inches, or 3 inches more than a yard. A 12-inch ruler is about 30 centimeters long. One inch is about 2.5 centimeters.

Volume

The standard unit of volume in the metric system is the liter. One liter is equal to 1,000 milliliters.

1 milliliter = 0.001 liter

1 liter = 1,000 milliliters

Abbreviate these volumes as follows:

1 milliliter = 1 ml

1 liter = 1 l

Comparisons to the U.S. system: One liter is a little more than a quart. A 1-cup measuring cup holds about 250 milliliters. A teaspoon is about 5 milliliters.

Mass (Weight)

The standard unit of mass in the metric system is the gram. One gram contains 1,000 milligrams. One kilogram is 1,000 grams.

1 milligram = 0.001 gram

1,000 milligrams = 1 gram

1 kilogram = 1,000 grams

Abbreviate these masses as follows:

1 milligram = 1 mg

1 gram = 1 g

1 kilogram = 1 kg

Comparisons to the U.S. system: A kilogram is 2.2 pounds. One pound is 454 grams. One ounce is 28 grams.

Temperature

Temperature is expressed in degrees Celsius in the metric system. The boiling point of water (at sea level) is 100° Celsius, or 100°C. The freezing point of water (at sea level) is 0°C. Room temperature is about 21°C. Human body temperature is 37°C.

Comparisons to the U.S. system: In the United States, we often report the weather, body temperature, and other temperature measurements in degrees Fahrenheit. The boiling point of water (at sea level) is 212° Fahrenheit, or 212°F. The freezing point of water (at sea level) is 32°F. Room temperature is about 70°F. Human body temperature is 98.6°F.

Conversions

Conversion factors allow you to change U.S. measures to metric measures. This table shows some of the more frequently used conversion factors. Read this table from left to right. For example, the first row tells you, "If you want centimeters, but you measured in inches, multiply (centimeters) by 2.5."

If You Want . . .	But You Measured In . . .	Multiply By (Approximate)
Centimeters	Inches	2.5
Meters	Feet	0.31
Milliliters	Fluid ounces	30.0
Milliliters	Tablespoons	15
Milliliters	Teaspoons	5
Milliliters	Cups	250
Liters	Pints	0.47
Liters	Quarts	0.95
Liters	Gallons	3.78
Grams	Ounces	28.3
Kilograms	Pounds	0.45

To convert degrees Fahrenheit to degrees Celsius, use this formula:

$$C = \tfrac{5}{9} (F - 32)$$

Example: To convert 50°F to °C, subtract 32 from 50. Multiply that answer by 5. Then divide that product by 9.

$$50 - 32 = 18$$
$$18 \times 5 = 90$$
$$90 \div 9 = 10°C$$

To convert degrees Celsius to degrees Fahrenheit, use this formula:

$$F = \tfrac{9}{5} C + 32$$

Example: To convert 30°C to °F, multiply 30 by 9. Divide that product by 5. Add 32 to your answer.

$$30 \times 9 = 270$$
$$270 \div 5 = 54$$
$$54 + 32 = 86°C$$

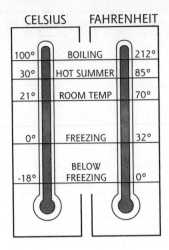

Constructing a Display

The purpose of a display is to communicate the project to others. That means showing what was done, how, and why. The display summarize the parts of the project (see the "What Must a Science Project Contain?" chapter in Part I) clearly, accurately, and briefly. The display cannot and should not show every idea that was considered, every piece of data that was collected, or every trial of every experiment. That information should be recorded in the logbook and shown along with the project. Instead, the display follows the format of a scientific paper. It delineates the purpose, materials, methods, and results, along with the conclusions drawn from them.

Many science fairs have strict requirements about the size and shape of the display. Many suggest a three-sided poster. The display board can be made of posterboard, laminated cardboard, plywood, pegboard, foamboard, or paneling—either taped or hinged together. Office supply stores often sell science project display kits, complete with premade, folding board and materials for lettering. Whatever materials you choose, make sure your display conforms to the rules set by your teacher or science fair committee.

The rules may allow some leeway in how display boards are presented. Often, students place the title and results of their experiment on the center panel. Goals, materials, methods, and conclusions appear on the two side panels. Materials from the experiment, demonstrations, models, and the logbook can be displayed on the table in front of the backboard. Do not display any materials that are potentially hazardous, spillable, or perishable. Do not display live animals. Plants are sometimes prohibited, also. Check your fair's rules.

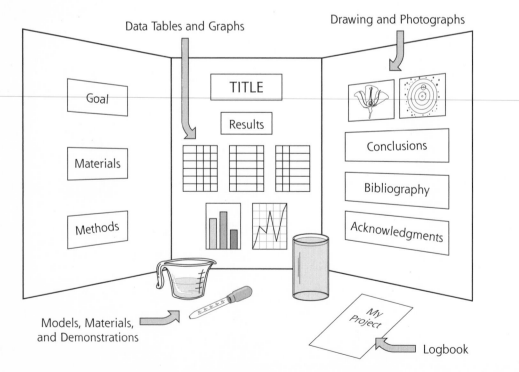

Although the judges at science fairs are most interested in the scientific process and content of a project, presentation does matter. Neatness is essential. Choose attractive colors for the display board, and make titles and type large and easy to read. Use drawings and photographs for two purposes:

- To show experimental methods and results
- To make the display visually interesting

Get creative. If borders, fonts, text boxes, and clip art help communicate your project effectively, use them. Style will never win over substance in a science project, but it can help a good project stand out from the rest.

Many science fairs ask students to stand beside their projects to explain their work to visitors and to answer questions from the judges. The rules here are

- Stand tall.
- Speak with confidence.
- Answer questions honestly and briefly.
- Admit mistakes and tell how you can correct them the next time you do a science project.
- Let your enthusiasm show.

Planning for Next Year

Does this sound familiar? "Okay, I admit it. This year I didn't start my science project early enough. I had trouble thinking of a question. I just picked the first one I found in a book, so I wasn't as interested in it as I should have been. I put off collecting data and didn't conduct several trials, so I wasn't able to average my data. I forgot to take photographs that would have made my display better. I made my graphs the night before the project was due, and I set them up wrong. If I had planned ahead, I would have had time to get help from the math teacher. If I had planned ahead . . ."

If that confession sounds like you or someone in your family, don't despair. Yes, we are all human, and procrastination is a common failing. The result may be that this year's project was less than satisfactory. Seldom, however, is this a "last chance" situation. Another science project opportunity will probably arise next year or the year after that, so now is the time to admit mistakes, learn from them, and begin preparation for a better effort the next time around.

A good way to get ahead is to keep a science journal and write in it frequently. Record any and all ideas: something you observe in nature, a question that comes to mind, or something you see on TV that sparks your interest. Or you might try a mini-experiment when you have some spare time, perhaps using one of the ideas in this book. Trying something and noting the result may lead you to more and better ideas to pursue in years to come. Consider, also, reviewing the "Go Easy," "Go," and "Go Far" procedures in this book to see whether any capture your interest. Starting now, you can get a head start on your outstanding science project for next year.